Lecture Notes in Computer Sci

Commenced Publication in 1973
Founding and Former Series Editors:
Gerhard Goos, Juris Hartmanis, and Jan van Leeuwen

Editorial Board

David Hutchison
  Lancaster University, UK
Takeo Kanade
  Carnegie Mellon University, Pittsburgh, PA, USA
Josef Kittler
  University of Surrey, Guildford, UK
Jon M. Kleinberg
  Cornell University, Ithaca, NY, USA
Alfred Kobsa
  University of California, Irvine, CA, USA
Friedemann Mattern
  ETH Zurich, Switzerland
John C. Mitchell
  Stanford University, CA, USA
Moni Naor
  Weizmann Institute of Science, Rehovot, Israel
Oscar Nierstrasz
  University of Bern, Switzerland
C. Pandu Rangan
  Indian Institute of Technology, Madras, India
Bernhard Steffen
  TU Dortmund University, Germany
Madhu Sudan
  Microsoft Research, Cambridge, MA, USA
Demetri Terzopoulos
  University of California, Los Angeles, CA, USA
Doug Tygar
  University of California, Berkeley, CA, USA
Gerhard Weikum
  Max Planck Institute for Informatics, Saarbruecken, Germany

Chris J. Mitchell   Allan Tomlinson (Eds.)

Trusted Systems

4th International Conference, INTRUST 2012
London, UK, December 17-18, 2012
Proceedings

 Springer

Volume Editors

Chris J. Mitchell
Allan Tomlinson
University of London, Information Security Group
Royal Holloway, Egham, Surrey TW20 0EX, UK
E-mail: me@chrismitchell.net, allan.tomlinson@rhul.ac.uk

ISSN 0302-9743   e-ISSN 1611-3349
ISBN 978-3-642-35370-3   e-ISBN 978-3-642-35371-0
DOI 10.1007/978-3-642-35371-0
Springer Heidelberg Dordrecht London New York

Library of Congress Control Number: Applied for

CR Subject Classification (1998): D.4.6, E.3, K.6.5, C.2, K.4.4, J.1, H.4

LNCS Sublibrary: SL 4 – Security and Cryptology

© Springer-Verlag Berlin Heidelberg 2012

This work is subject to copyright. All rights are reserved, whether the whole or part of the material is concerned, specifically the rights of translation, reprinting, re-use of illustrations, recitation, broadcasting, reproduction on microfilms or in any other way, and storage in data banks. Duplication of this publication or parts thereof is permitted only under the provisions of the German Copyright Law of September 9, 1965, in its current version, and permission for use must always be obtained from Springer. Violations are liable to prosecution under the German Copyright Law.
The use of general descriptive names, registered names, trademarks, etc. in this publication does not imply, even in the absence of a specific statement, that such names are exempt from the relevant protective laws and regulations and therefore free for general use.

Typesetting: Camera-ready by author, data conversion by Scientific Publishing Services, Chennai, India

Printed on acid-free paper

Springer is part of Springer Science+Business Media (www.springer.com)

Preface

This volume contains ten papers presented and discussed at the InTrust 2012 conference, held at Royal Holloway, University of London, Egham, UK, in December 2012. InTrust 2012 was the fourth international conference on the theory, technologies, and applications of trusted systems. It was devoted to all aspects of trusted computing systems, including trusted modules, platforms, networks, services, and applications, from their fundamental features and functionality to design principles, architecture, and implementation technologies. The goal of the conference was to bring academic and industrial researchers, designers, and implementers together with end-users of trusted systems, in order to foster the exchange of ideas in this challenging and fruitful area.

InTrust 2012 built on the three previous successful conferences in the series, held in Beijing in December 2009, December 2010, and November 2011. The proceedings of INTRUST 2009, containing 16 papers, were published in volume 6163 of the *Lecture Notes in Computer Science*. The proceedings of INTRUST 2010, containing 23 papers, were published in volume 6802 of the *Lecture Notes in Computer Science*. The proceedings of INTRUST 2011, containing 21 papers, were published in volume 7222 of the *Lecture Notes in Computer Science*.

The program of InTrust 2012 was made up of six contributed papers, four invited keynote presentations, and a panel session. Short papers by three of the invited speakers (Javier Lopez, Christof Paar, and Mark Ryan) are included in the proceedings; the fourth keynote speaker, Paul Waller (CESG, UK) gave a talk entitled "Secure By Default — Assuring and Evolving Platform Security". The panel session was organized and led by Shin'ichiro Matsuo (NICT, Japan), and a short paper which formed the basis for the session is included in the proceedings. Panel session participants included Nicolai Kuntze (Fraunhofer Institute), Graeme Proudler (Hewlett-Packard Laboratories and TCG), Charles Brookson (Chair of GSMA SG and ETSI OCG), and Kenny Paterson (Royal Holloway, University of London). Special thanks are due to the keynote speakers, the panel session organizer, and the panel session participants.

The contributed papers were selected out of 19 submissions from 14 countries, giving an acceptance rate of 32%. All submissions were blind-reviewed, i.e., the Program Committee members provided reviews on anonymous submissions. The refereeing process was rigorous, involving three (and sometimes more) independent reports being prepared for each submission. The individual reviewing phase was followed by discussions about the papers, which contributed greatly to the quality of the final selection. A number of accepted papers were shepherded by Program Committee members in order to make sure the review comments were properly addressed. We are very grateful to our hard-working and distinguished Program Committee for doing such an excellent job in a timely fashion.

We owe a huge debt to Liqun Chen for acting as General Chair and providing a constant source of helpful advice and encouragement; without her this event would not have taken place. We would also like to thank the conference Steering Committee led by Yongfei Han for valuable guidance and assistance, and Emma Mosley for managing the arrangements at Royal Holloway. Thanks are also due to EasyChair for providing the submission and review Web server.

On behalf of the conference organization and participants, we would like to express our appreciation to Singapore Management University and the Information Security Group at Royal Holloway for their generous sponsorship of this event.

We would also like to thank the authors who submitted their papers to the InTrust 2012 conference, the external referees, and, last but not least, the attendees of the conference. Authors of accepted papers are thanked again for revising their papers according to the feedback from the conference participants. The revised versions were not formally checked by the Program Committee, so the authors bear full responsibility for their contents. We thank the staff at Springer for their help with producing the proceedings.

October 2012   Chris Mitchell
Allan Tomlison

InTrust 2012

The 4th International Conference on Trusted Systems
Royal Holloway, University of London, Egham, UK
December 17–18, 2012

Honorary Chairs

Yongfei Han	BJUT and ONETS, China
Moti Yung	Google and Columbia University, USA

General Chairs

Liqun Chen	Hewlett-Packard Laboratories, UK
Chris Mitchell	Royal Holloway, University of London, UK
Allan Tomlinson	Royal Holloway, University of London, UK

Program Chairs

Chris Mitchell	Royal Holloway, University of London, UK
Allan Tomlinson	Royal Holloway, University of London, UK

Program Committee

Endre Bangerter	Bern University of Applied Sciences, Switzerland
Feng Bao	I2R, Singapore
Giampaolo Bella	Università di Catania, Italy
Haibo Chen	Shanghai Jiao Tong University, China
Zhong Chen	Peking University, China
Kurt Dietrich	Graz University of Technology, Austria
Xuhua Ding	Singapore Management University, Singapore
Loic Duflot	SGDN, France
Dieter Gollmann	Hamburg University of Technology, Germany
David Grawrock	Intel, USA
Sigrid Guergens	Fraunhofer Institute for Secure Information Technology, Germany
Dirk Kuhlmann	HP Laboratories, UK
Xuejia Lai	Shanghai Jiao Tong University, China
Jiangtao Li	Intel, USA
Shujun Li	University of Konstanz, Germany
Peter Lipp	Graz University of Technology, Austria
Javier Lopez	University of Malaga, Spain

Andrew Martin	University of Oxford, UK
Shin'ichiro Matsuo	NICT, Japan
Yi Mu	University of Wollongong, Australia
David Naccache	ENS, France
Kenny Paterson	Royal Holloway, University of London, UK
Graeme Proudler	HP Laboratories, UK
Sihan Qing	Chinese Academy of Sciences, China
Scott Rotondo	Oracle, USA
Mark Ryan	University of Birmingham, UK
Willy Susilo	University of Wollongong, Australia
Qiang Tang	University of Twente, The Netherlands
Claire Vishik	Intel, USA
Jian Weng	Jinan University, China
Shouhuai Xu	UTSA, USA
Rui Xue	Chinese Academy of Sciences, China
Xinwen Zhang	Huawei Research Center, USA
Yongbin Zhou	Chinese Academy of Sciences, China
Liehuang Zhu	Beijing Institute of Technology, China
Yan Zhu	Peking University, China

Steering Committee

Yongfei Han	BJUT and ONETS, China
Moti Yung	Google and Columbia University, USA
Liqun Chen	HP Laboratories, UK
Robert Deng	SMU, Singapore
Chris Mitchell	RHUL, UK

External Reviewers

Sergiu Bursuc	Weiliang Luo
Liqun Chen	Li Yang
Ulrich Fiedler	Rui Zhang
Qi Li	Qingji Zheng
Lei Liu	

Table of Contents

Session 6: Embedded Security

Automatic Analysis
of Security Properties of the TPM

Mark D. Ryan

School of Computer Science, University of Birmingham, UK

1   The TPM and Some Attacks

The trusted platform module (TPM) is a hardware chip designed to enable commodity computers to achieve greater levels of security than is possible in software alone. There are 300 million TPMs currently in existence, mostly in high-end laptops, but now increasingly in desktops and servers. Application software such as Microsoft's BitLocker and HP's ProtectTools use the TPM in order to guarantee security properties. The TPM specification is an industry standard [1] and an ISO/IEC standard [2] co-ordinated by the Trusted Computing Group.

In the last few years, several vulnerabilities in the TPM API have been discovered, particularly in relation to secrecy and authentication properties.

Gürgens *et al.* [3] describe how an attacker can in some circumstances illegitimately obtain a certificate on a TPM key of his choice. Other attacks on the TPM include offline dictionary attacks on the passwords or authdata used to secure access to keys [4], and attacks exploiting the fact that the same authdata can be shared between users [5]. There is a further known attack whereby an attacker intercepts a message, aiming to cause the legitimate user to issue another one, and then causes both to be received, resulting in the message being processed twice [6].

2   Verification

The attacks mentioned above highlight the necessity of formal analysis of the API specification of the TPM. We have adapted ProVerif [7] for this purpose.

2.1   Authentication Protocols in the TPM

In [8], we model a collection of four TPM commands, concentrating on the authentication mechanisms. We identify security properties which we argue are central to correct and coherent design of the API. We formalise these properties for our fragment, and using ProVerif, we rediscover some known attacks on the API and some new variations on them. We discuss some fixes to the API, and prove our security properties for the modified API.

C.J. Mitchell and A. Tomlinson (Eds.): INTRUST 2012, LNCS 7711, pp. 1–4, 2012.
© Springer-Verlag Berlin Heidelberg 2012

2.2   Protocols Based on PCRs

The *platform configuration registers* (PCRs) of the TPM represent a particular challenge to formal analysis because they represent a global state that is shared between TPM command invocations. In other words, the result of executing a command depends on the current PCR values, which depend on the results of previous commands.

In [9], we model a fragment of the TPM including key management and key usage commands, taking into account operations for setting and reading PCRs, in first-order logic. Our modelling and verification techniques follow previous work by Weidenbach using SPASS [10] and in particular Blanchet using the tool ProVerif [7]. In this approach one generally considers a unary predicate att(*m*) for modelling that the adversary has knowledge of message *m*. To allow ourselves to model a PCR, we consider a binary predicate att; the fact att(*u, m*) means that the attacker can reach a state where the PCR has value *u* and where the attacker knows message *m*. Unfortunately, the resolution algorithms of SPASS and ProVerif quickly encounter non-termination problems when we run them on a model of the TPM using such binary predicates. We therefore prove that for a class of *k-stable* clauses, we can safely bound the number of times a PCR may be extended between two resets: we show that if there exists an attack then there exists also an attack that only considers such "small" PCR values. This allows us to specialise the clauses of our model in a way such that ProVerif terminates.

We also give syntactic conditions that are sufficient to show that the clauses in the two case studies we consider are *k*-stable. Our first case study is a simplified version of the *BitLocker protocol* [11], focusing on the usage of the PCR to build a *chain of trust*. The second protocol is a secure *envelope protocol* [12]. Both protocols crucially rely on the use of the PCR and we are able to prove their correctness using ProVerif.

2.3   The StatVerif Tool

In [13], we generalise the method described above. We present StatVerif, which is an extension of the ProVerif process language with constructs that allow one to directly model global mutable state. This approach allows us to build on ProVerif's existing successes. More precisely,

- We extend the ProVerif process calculus with explicit state, including assignments, and provide its operational semantics.
- We extend the ProVerif compiler, which takes processes written in the process language, and produces Horn clauses. Our translation is carefully engineered to avoid the false attacks mentioned in the paper.
- We prove the correctness of the extended compiler; that is, we show that attacks are not lost. Therefore, a security proof at the clause level implies a proof at the process calculus level.
- We illustrate out method on two examples: a small hardware security device, and a contract signing protocol. We are able to prove their desired properties automatically.

2.4   Modelling Dynamic Measurement and Protected Execution

The most interesting and powerful feature of the TPM is its ability to associate secrets (such as keys or other data) with particular software binaries, in a way that guarantees to a remote party that only the specified software has access to the secrets.

The TPM and the main processor together offer the facility of running a self-contained piece of software in an isolated environment. This code runs independently of the rest of the system, while enjoying access to the protected secrets. The code is measured and the measurement is extended into PCRs as it is loaded, and during loading and execution the processor disables the facilities that would be required by an attacker to alter the code.

The secrets are encrypted with a public key such that the corresponding secret key is known only to the TPM. The TPM allows decryption with the secret key only if the PCR values match the measurement of the intended software.

In [14], we propose a formal model of protected execution that allows us to reason about the secrecy of data sealed to a piece of software and the correctness of that software. We propose an attacker who can perform arbitrary private computation as well as using all the facilities available to the defender, including using dynamic measurement to execute either the code available to the defender or code chosen by the attacker. We use these models to analyse the security of pieces of software which use protected execution.

Our models cannot be analysed with currently available tools, because the potentially unlimited use of dynamic measurement prevents termination. We therefore prove a transformation which allows us to set an upper bound on the number of uses of dynamic measurement. Given some reasonable constraints on the initial data, which we justify, we show that no attacks are lost in this transformation. We can therefore take models which are not tractable with current tools and transform them to equivalent models that can be analysed automatically.

Drawing on Flicker [15], which uses dynamic measurement to provide isolated execution of security-sensitive code, we demonstrate a tool-chain that uses this transformation to prove the secrecy of security-sensitive code. As well as a running example, we take two practical examples from Flicker and use them as case studies.

3   Conclusions

The work we report has made significant inroads in analysing the TPM, but there is still a lot more that can be done. We have considered only a relatively small fraction of approximately 120 commands of the TPM. Other data structures within the TPM, such as its key tables, monotonic counters and saved contexts, should also be modelled.

Although the abstractions we found in [9] and [14] were sufficient to ensure termination of the resolution algorithm of ProVerif and StatVerif, it is not clear that such abstractions can always be found, and it is not known how to prove them automatically.

References

1. Trusted Computing Group: TPM Specification version 1.2. Parts 1–3 (2007), http://www.trustedcomputinggroup.org/resources/tpm_main_specification
2. ISO/IEC: ISO/IEC PAS DIS 11889: Information technology – Security techniques – Trusted platform module
3. Gürgens, S., Rudolph, C., Scheuermann, D., Atts, M., Plaga, R.: Security Evaluation of Scenarios Based on the TCG's TPM Specification. In: Biskup, J., López, J. (eds.) ESORICS 2007. LNCS, vol. 4734, pp. 438–453. Springer, Heidelberg (2007)
4. Chen, L., Ryan, M.D.: Offline dictionary attack on TCG TPM weak authorisation data, and solution. In: Grawrock, D., Reimer, H., Sadeghi, A., Vishik, C. (eds.) Future of Trust in Computing. Vieweg & Teubner (2008)
5. Chen, L., Ryan, M.D.: Attack, Solution and Verification for Shared Authorisation Data in TCG TPM. In: Degano, P., Guttman, J.D. (eds.) FAST 2009. LNCS, vol. 5983, pp. 201–216. Springer, Heidelberg (2010)
6. Bruschi, D., Cavallaro, L., Lanzi, A., Monga, M.: Replay attack in TCG specification and solution. In: ACSAC 2005: Proceedings of the 21st Annual Computer Security Applications Conference, pp. 127–137. IEEE Computer Society, Washington, DC (2005)
7. Blanchet, B.: An efficient cryptographic protocol verifier based on Prolog rules. In: Schneider, S. (ed.) 14th IEEE Computer Security Foundations Workshop, pp. 82–96. IEEE Computer Society Press, Cape Breton (2001)
8. Delaune, S., Kremer, S., Ryan, M.D., Steel, G.: A Formal Analysis of Authentication in the TPM. In: Degano, P., Etalle, S., Guttman, J. D. (eds.) FAST 2010. LNCS, vol. 6561, pp. 111–125. Springer, Heidelberg (2011)
9. Delaune, S., Kremer, S., Ryan, M.D., Steel, G.: Formal analysis of protocols based on TPM state registers. In: [16], pp. 66–80
10. Weidenbach, C.: Towards an Automatic Analysis of Security Protocols in First-Order Logic. In: Ganzinger, H. (ed.) CADE 1999. LNCS (LNAI), vol. 1632, pp. 314–328. Springer, Heidelberg (1999)
11. Microsoft: BitLocker FAQ, http://technet.microsoft.com/en-us/library/ee449438(WS.10).aspx
12. Ables, K., Ryan, M.D.: Escrowed Data and the Digital Envelope. In: Acquisti, A., Smith, S.W., Sadeghi, A.-R. (eds.) TRUST 2010. LNCS, vol. 6101, pp. 246–256. Springer, Heidelberg (2010)
13. Arapinis, M., Ritter, E., Ryan, M.D.: StatVerif: Verification of stateful processes. In: [16], pp. 33–47
14. Xu, S., Batten, I., Ryan, M.: Dynamic measurement and protected execution: model and analysis. Paper in Preparation
15. McCune, J.M., Parno, B., Perrig, A., Reiter, M.K., Isozaki, H.: Flicker: An execution infrastructure for tcb minimization. In: Proceedings of the ACM European Conference in Computer Systems (EuroSys) (April 2008)
16. Proceedings of the 24th IEEE Computer Security Foundations Symposium, CSF 2011, June 27-29, IEEE Computer Society, Cernay-la-Ville, France (2011)

Stamp and Extend –
Instant But Undeniable Timestamping Based on Lazy Trees*

Łukasz Krzywiecki, Przemysław Kubiak, and Mirosław Kutyłowski

Faculty of Fundamental Problems of Technology, Wrocław University of Technology
{lukasz.krzywiecki,przemyslaw.kubiak,
miroslaw.kutylowski}@pwr.wroc.pl

Abstract. We present a Stamp&Extend time-stamping scheme based on linking via modified creation of Schnorr signatures. The scheme is based on lazy construction of a tree of signatures.

Stamp&Extend returns a timestamp immediately after the request, unlike the schemes based on the concept of timestamping rounds. Despite the fact that all timestamps are linearly linked, verification of a timestamp requires a logarithmic number of steps with respect to the chain length. An extra feature of the scheme is that any attempt to forge a timestamp by the Time Stamping Authority (TSA) results in revealing its secret key, providing an undeniable cryptographic evidence of misbehavior of TSA.

Breaking Stamp&Extend requires not only breaking Schnorr signatures, but to some extend also breaking Pedersen commitments.

Keywords: timestamping, undeniability, forgery evidence, Schnorr signature.

1 Introduction

1.1 Legal Background

Timestamping is one of the very basic services that are necessary for electronic document flow. According to a recent legal definition [1]:

'electronic time stamp' means data in electronic form which binds other electronic data to a particular time establishing evidence that these data existed at that time.

Time stamps are perhaps as important as digital signatures for future applications: while a digital signature provides guarantees for document origin and its approval by the signatory, it does not prove when the signature was created. However, signing time is crucial for the legal consequences of a signed document. This concerns not only such trivial cases as documentation for online financial operations (e.g. on a stock exchange), but also administrative procedures, where a party participating in a procedure has a limited period of time to perform a legally valid action. Importance of timestamping was recognized in this legal environment – it was mentioned already by European Directive concerning electronic signature a decade ago [2].

---

* The paper is partially supported by Foundation for Polish Science, MISTRZ project.

C.J. Mitchell and A. Tomlinson (Eds.): INTRUST 2012, LNCS 7711, pp. 5–24, 2012.
© Springer-Verlag Berlin Heidelberg 2012

Recently, European Commission proposed a new regulation concerning electronic identification and trust services [1]. Time-stamping is one of the main elements of the proposed framework. The proposal states that electronic time-stamp *shall not be denied legal effect and admissibility as evidence in legal proceedings solely on the grounds that it is in electronic form*. In case of qualified time-stamps (i.e. the time-stamps issued by qualified service providers), *electronic time stamp shall enjoy a legal presumption of ensuring the time it indicates and the integrity of the data to which the time is bound*. Thereby, electronic time-stamps will become an important legal institution.

New laws concerning timestamping means facilitating use of electronic documents in legal proceedings. On the other hand, without a flawless technical framework electronic time-stamps may become a powerful tool for electronic frauds. This has not been so important so far, since it was not compulsory to accept electronic time-stamps in legal proceedings. Designing time-stamping systems must also take into account possibility of malicious activities of all participants of the process, including in particular *qualified service providers*, and the threat of breaking cryptographic schemes. Introducing a new technology into a legal framework should be coupled with effective e-forensics techniques. Possible legal conflicts concerning timestamps should be solvable on technical grounds. Otherwise, this technology can be used to create *time machines* in the legal framework. Namely, a party having backdoors to the timestamping services would have an opportunity to perfectly backdate electronic documents.

1.2 Certification and Secure Timestamping Devices

An idea which is dominant in existing implementations is to rely on special purpose *secure timestamping devices* - just like in the case of electronic signatures and *secure signature creation devices* holding private signing keys. As in case of signature creation devices, technical security and resistance to manipulations should be checked during certification process, where details are disclosed to trusted certification bodies. While certification process is a very important element of efforts for providing security, one has to keep in mind that it does not necessarily guarantee elimination of backdoors. Certification process reduces significantly the amount of design mistakes enforcing a rigorous design and implementation, as well as formulation of design goals and product features. However, this is only a process of checking of some properties against a certain list that may simply ignore or overlook some important issues.

Providing guarantees for security of *timestamping devices* is significantly harder than in case of *signature creation devices*. Indeed, in the last case the owner of the device has very strong reasons to protect it against attacks. Namely, compromising the signing key open doors to creation of perfect signatures on behalf of the attacked person. The situation might be very different for a TSA – it may attempt to retrieve the keys stored in the device in order to be able to backdate certain documents. We have to be aware of the fact that organized crime might be interested in controlling TSA in order to make perfect frauds efficiently.

The lessons learned from early e-voting implementations show that we should be very careful when entrusting blindly black box devices. Today, after disasters with e-voting machines in USA and Netherlands (which were due to blind trust to manufacturers and their products), it is much harder to convince the users to such solutions. There should be a strong argument behind the construction of timestamps that is not based solely on the assumption that the timestamping service provider and the manufacturer are honest and competent. Even if they are, there might be third parties that have better cryptographic and technical knowledge as well as better resources enabling them to exploit some unknown weaknesses of the devices.

1.3 Undeniable Timestamping – Related Work

Round Schemes. The very first constructions of undeniable timestamps have been presented in [3], [4]. The basic idea is simple: there is a service provider, TSA, that issues timestamps on demand. TSA builds a database secured with cryptographic means so that it allows append operation but does not allow insert operations and modifications of past records.

The basic structure here is a linear chain of hashes: the next element in the chain contains a signature of TSA not only on the digital data to be stamped, but also on the hash of the previous element in the chain. Therefore, it is impossible to change an element of the chain: any manipulation would change its hash value and therefore disconnect it from its successor. However, hash chains have a serious disadvantage. Since the hash chain is anchored at its initial element (confirmed by a third party or published), while checking a timestamp it is necessary to perform a number of operations that is linear in the number of timestamps. Obviously such a solution in not scalable and can be used only in small systems.

The idea to overcome this problem is to split time into rounds and link only data between the rounds. Within a round, TSA is executing a procedure that finally delivers a single value to be incorporated in a linear chain connecting the rounds. For making a round, different techniques has been proposed. One solution is to use one-way accumulators [5]: all requests gathered during one round are accumulated into a single hash value, and at the end of the round each requester receives a compact proof (i.e., a timestamp) that her/his request is included in the hash value. The underlying hash function is build upon exponentiation modulo a product of two strong primes that have the same length. The scheme [5] is a distributed one, with key generation procedure distributed as well (the latter is pretty complicated, see e.g., [6]), or alternatively, with centralized generation of the modulus (but then the central server must be trusted).

An alternative solution is to generate a single aggregated signature for all data submitted during a single round (see e.g., scheme [7] build upon bilinear maps).

However, majority of proposals use a kind of Merkle tree generated for the timestamped values located at leaves of the tree. This provides both undeniability as well as proofs of presence in the tree with a given root having logarithmic lengths. The idea is very simple, nevertheless there are some fine issues concerning the scheme:

- While it is obvious that a cryptographic hash function should be used to generate labels of the tree nodes, it is not completely clear which properties are really necessary. However, after formulating the requirements, the schemes can be examined via reduction proofs: finding a relationship between breaking a timestamping scheme and breaking some standard security assumption. For considerations of this kind see e.g. papers [8], [9],[10],[11],[12].

- It is not only hash function that matters – it turns out that carefully tailored construction of hash trees may improve efficiency of the scheme – see e.g. a design based on skewed trees [13]. Moreover, trees are not necessarily the best data structure. Essentially, the same chain of trust can be built in a directed acyclic simple graph with a single sink – see e.g. a solution based on skip lists [14].

Instant Timestamping. The main *drawback of the round approach* is improving scalability at the price of response time: instead of one-stop-shop there is an interaction between the requester and TSA extended until the end of the round. That is, *to obtain a timestamp the requester must wait for the end of the round.*

A notable exception among round-based schemes is the protocol from [15]: hashes of the requests are generated *in advance*, using chameleon hash function. Then a Merkle tree is built from the leaves being these hash-values produced in advance, and the root of the tree becomes the public commitment that can be used to authenticate the future timestamps. To avoid frauds the scheme from [15] distributes the trapdoor for the chameleon hash function among a few servers. Consequently, clients' requests are answered immediately, but operational costs of the service are increased by using a distributed protocol to generate preimages for the chameleon hashes, which is necessary to answer the requests.

1.4 Our Contribution

We change the approach presented in [15]. Instead from making commitments to the hashes of the future requests, the protocol presented below makes commitments to the randomness that will be used to generate signatures under answers to the requests. The crucial point is that if the same randomness is used to sign two different requests, then the private signature key leaks from TSA. Consequently, instead of designing a distributed system ([5], [15]) we propose a cheaper centralized one, which is deterred from misbehavior by the threat of the signature key leak. The idea of deterrence by key leak was utilized in a stand-alone signature protocol [16]. However, the scheme presented in [16] is highly inefficient – a single signature must be composed of more than *eighty* Rabin-Williams sub-signatures.

Moreover, the commitments to the randomness are made gradually during the protocol execution, when the currently submitted requests are served. Since the randomness used for signature generation is independent from the hash values resulting from future requests, a separate setup phase for building a Merkle tree is no longer needed. For each timestamp generated, two commitments are prepared for a future use (i.e., a timestamp makes links to *future* nodes, and these links are independent from hash values resulting from the requests the links will be used for). In this way some binary tree is gradually created (cf. Fig. 2 on page 14), what shall be utilized by the timestamp verification procedure. The size of the tree is limited only by users' expectations to timestamp verification time, thus the size is not predetermined like in the scheme [15]. If size of the tree becomes too big, the private key material of TSA may be destroyed (see Subsect. 3.3) and a new tree could be initialized.

To sum up, we propose a Stamp&Extend time stamping scheme that has the following properties:

- the Time Stamping Authority is centralized, i.e., it can be run on a single server,
- interaction between the requester and the centralized TSA is limited to the request and its immediate response; there is no need to wait for the end of a round,
- every two timestamps issued by the same TSA are comparable with respect to the order they were requested (as in the simple linear linking scheme),
- communication complexity from TSA to the requester is logarithmic in the number of timestamps issued so far, and at the same time computational complexity for issuing a timestamp is constant,
- issuing a backdated document exposes the signing key of TSA,
- the main security features are based on hardness of discrete logarithm problem and on non-repudiation of Schnorr signatures.

1.5 Security Requirements

To correctly describe the idea of deterrence mentioned in Subsect. 1.4 we shall first explain what forgery means in case of the Stamp&Extend scheme.

The scheme is build upon the classical protocol, i.e., upon the linear chain of hashes: the verification procedure (see Algorithm 4) checks if the timestamp verified has the link to its predecessor in the chain. If the link is absent the timestamp is rejected and TSA is caught cheating (TSA signs each timestamp generated). Ill-formedness of a timestamp is not penalized in our scheme by TSA's private key leak, however any later efforts of TSA to replace the ill-formed timestamp *are* penalized.

As mentioned in Subsect. 1.4, we focus on TSA signatures: the linear chain structure is augmented with a system of commitments that are commitments to randomness used in the signatures. Each commitment corresponds to a single position in the linear chain of timestamps, and the system of commitments has the form of a binary tree (such a form accelerates verification of a single commitment). The two structures (the linear chain and the binary tree) are fused together – see Fig. 2 on page 14, and each commitment in fact *determines* the in-chain position of a timestamp, for whose signature the committed randomness is used for. Therefore, even if some positions are left empty by the TSA, i.e., even if the malicious authority makes a gap for a future use and starts a new chain on some forward position, the new and the old chain are glued together by the binary structure of commitments. Hence the term *alleged chain* is justified and may be used in the following definition:

Definition 1. *By a forgery we mean issuing two timestamps for the same position of the alleged chain.*

The Stamp & Extend scheme must ensure that:

1. The system of commitments does not weaken the signature scheme used by TSA.
2. The deterrence mechanism is efficient, i.e. in case of a forgery the private signature key of TSA leaks with a non-negligible probability.

Condition 1 is addressed by considering external adversaries – cf. Definition 3 and Theorem 2 in Subsect. 3.1. Condition 2 is addressed by Theorem 3 from Subsect. 3.2.

2 Stamp and Extend Protocol

2.1 Protocol's Building Blocks

Schnorr Signatures. Our construction is based on Schnorr signatures [17], [18, Subsect.4.2.3]. Let us recall the scheme briefly. Let G be a group of a prime order q for which Discrete Logarithm Problem (DLP) is hard. Let g be a fixed generator of this group.

Private key of a user u is a number $x \in [1, q-1]$ chosen at random. The corresponding public key is an element of group G computed as $y := g^x$.

For signature creation we use a cryptographic hash function H. A signature of a message M is created as follows:

1. the signer chooses an integer $k \in [1, q-1]$ uniformly at random,
2. $r := g^k$,
3. $e := H(M \| r)$ ($\|$ stands for concatenation),
4. $s := (k - xe) \bmod q$,
5. output signature (e, s).

Verification of this signature is performed as follows:

1. $r' := g^s \cdot y^e$,
2. $e' := H(M \| r')$,
3. if $e = e'$ then return `true`, otherwise return `false`.

The Schnorr signature scheme is very elegant and simple. The main disadvantage of Schnorr signatures was a US patent [19], which encouraged manufacturers to implement other patent-free algorithms based on DLP. This situation has changed, as the patent [19] expired in 2008. For smart cards there is another disadvantage: the computation of r has to be done on the card before the message M is hashed. As hashing is executed typically outside the card, this increases the number of messages exchanged with the card. In our case this is not a problem, as we aim to create Schnorr signatures on a server.

Pedersen Commitments [20]. Let G be group of prime order q for which DLP is hard. Let g, h be generators of G such that $\log_g h$ is not known to anybody. Commitment c to k is obtained by choosing $\ell \in \{0, 1, \ldots, q-1\}$ uniformly at random and assigning:

$$c := g^k \cdot h^\ell.$$

The commitment can be later opened by the commiter by revealing k and ℓ. Commitment c reveals no information about k. Moreover, opening the commitment c to a k' such that $k' \neq k$ reveals the discrete logarithm $\log_g h$. Therefore it is infeasible to replace k by k'.

Actors	: TSA
Input	: group G of prime order q, generators g, h of G such that $\log_g h$ is not known to anybody
Output	: public key y, private key x, pair of starting parameters (k_1, ℓ_1), a Pedersen commitment c_1

1 for (k_1, ℓ_1) **begin**
2   choose $x \in \{1, 2, \ldots, q-1\}$ uniformly at random
3      $y := g^x$
4   **return** x as the private signing key
5   **return** and export y as the public signing key
6   choose $k_1, \ell_1 \in \{0, 1, \ldots, q-1\}$ uniformly at random
7      $c_1 := g^{k_1} h^{\ell_1}$
8   **return** (k_1, ℓ_1) as the first pair of private timestamping parameters
9   **return** and export c_1 as the public commitment for the first timestamp

Algorithm 1: Setup of keys for TSA.

2.2 The Protocol

Initialization. When starting a TSA the first step to do is to generate its public and private parameters. Before we do it, we have to choose a group G of a prime order, say q, where DLP is hard. We shall also use a secure hash function H. Setup of keys for TSA is depicted by Algorithm 1 .

After the keys are generated, it is necessary to confirm public parameters by issuing certificate(s) $Cert$ (see Algorithm 2). A standard form of publishing $Cert$ has to be chosen (e.g. publishing in a newspaper) so that the keys cannot be changed afterwards.

Creating Timestamps. TSA stores the following data during protocol execution:

- the index of the last timestamp issued $i - 1$,
- a private list P of pairs of exponents $[(k_i, \ell_i), \ldots, (k_{2i-1}, \ell_{2i-1})]$
- a public file C with the list of Pedersen commitments $[c_1, \ldots, c_{2i-1}]$,
- a public file HS that includes an initial value HS_0 (which is the certificate of TSA) and elements $HS_j = (T_j, H_j)$ for $j = 1, \ldots, i - 1$, where T_j is the jth timestamp and H_j is the corresponding timestamped value (i.e. a hash value together with identifier of the hash function used [21]).

Creation of the ith timestamp (see Algorithm 3) requires using c_i as well as *issuing two additional commitments* c_{2i}, c_{2i+1} and storing them in C. The list $C = [c_1, c_2, c_3, c_4, \ldots, c_7, \ldots, c_{2i}, c_{2i+1}]$ may be perceived as a list of consecutive layers of a binary tree (the currently bottom layer may not be completed):

$$C = [\{c_1\}, \{c_2, c_3\}, \{c_4, \ldots, c_7\}, \ldots, \{c_{2 \cdot 2^{\lfloor \log_2 i \rfloor}}, \ldots, c_{2i}, c_{2i+1}\}]$$

By making a signature of record (1), which contains the values c_{2i}, c_{2i+1}, TSA creates an authentication link from c_i to the nodes c_{2i}, c_{2i+1} (note that c_i is a commitment to the randomness used in the signature of (1)). The sequence of records (2) is in fact a kind of authentication path from the node c_i to the root c_1. The procedure is additionally illustrated by Fig. 1 on page 13 .

Actors : TSA, Certification Authority (CA)
Input : public signing key y, initial commitment c_1
Output : a certificate $Cert$ for y and c_1

1 **begin**
2   CA generates a digital certificate $Cert$ for y and c_1 in a standard way
3   CA publishes $Cert$
4   TSA initializes HS as the list $[HS_0]$, where $HS_0 = Cert$

Algorithm 2: Generating certificates for TSA.

Actors : TSA, a requester
Input :

- index $i - 1$ of the last timestamp issued
- list $C = [c_1, \ldots, c_{2i-1}]$ of Pedersen commitments
- list $P = [(k_i, \ell_i), \ldots, (k_{2i-1}, \ell_{2i-1})]$ of pairs of unused private exponents
- list HS including HS_0 and elements $HS_j = (T_j, H_j)$ for $j = 1, \ldots, i - 1$
- value H_i to be timestamped delivered by the requester

Output : updated: index i and lists C, P, HS

1 **begin**
2   choose $k_{2i}, \ell_{2i}, k_{2i+1}, \ell_{2i+1} \in \{0, 1, \ldots, q - 1\}$ uniformly at random
3     $c_{2i} := g^{k_{2i}} h^{\ell_{2i}}, \quad c_{2i+1} := g^{k_{2i+1}} h^{\ell_{2i+1}}$
4   append c_{2i}, c_{2i+1} to C
5     $k := k_i$
6   remove (k_i, ℓ_i) from P, append $(k_{2i}, \ell_{2i}), (k_{2i+1}, \ell_{2i+1})$ to P
7   create Schnorr signature S_i using random parameter k from line 5 for the following "message":

$$(H(HS_{i-1}), H_i, c_{2i}, c_{2i+1}, \ell_i, i), \tag{1}$$

    where $H()$ is cryptographically secure hash function used by TSA
8   define the ith timestamp as $T_i := (S_i, \ell_i, i)$ `/* note that one of the exponents for commitment` c_i `is revealed in the timestamp */`
9   append (T_i, H_i) to list HS as the last element HS_i `/* note that HS and` C `allow to reconstruct completely the message (1) */`
10   return index i to the requester
11   **alternatively**: return the following sequence of records to the requester

$$(S_j, H(HS_{j-1}), H_j, c_{2j}, c_{2j+1}, \ell_j, j) \tag{2}$$

    for $j = \lfloor i/2^\alpha \rfloor$, where $\alpha = 0, 1, \ldots, \lfloor \log_2 i \rfloor$.

Algorithm 3: Creating a timestamp by TSA.

Checking Timestamps. Timestamp verification can be executed according to Algorithm 4 given on page 14 .

Note that immediate access to C and real-time execution of line 8 of Algorithm 4 is not necessary. If the requester of a timestamp receives a sequence of records (2) for

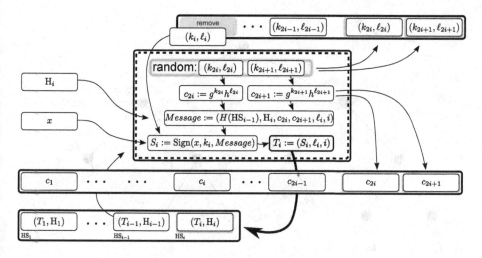

Fig. 1. Creation of the i-th timestamp

$j = \lfloor i/2^{\alpha} \rfloor$, where $\alpha = 0, 1, \ldots, \lfloor \log_2 i \rfloor$, and all signatures S_j are correct, then these signatures contain a kind of declaration to corresponding commitments c_j available to the public. The declarations are $c'_j = g^{e_j} y^{s_j} h^{\ell_j}$ – note that ℓ_j as well as indexes j are included in the signed data of the corresponding records (1). Accordingly, if TSA is cheating and records (2) contain at least one false declaration to value c_j, then it would be provably evident due to corresponding signature S_j: Note that if the sequence of declarations

$$c'_i, c'_{\lfloor i/2 \rfloor}, \ldots, c'_{\lfloor i/2^{\lfloor \log_2 i \rfloor - 2} \rfloor}, c'_{\lfloor i/2^{\lfloor \log_2 i \rfloor - 1} \rfloor}, c_1$$

is different from the publicly available sequence of commitments

$$c_i, c_{\lfloor i/2 \rfloor}, \ldots, c_{\lfloor i/2^{\lfloor \log_2 i \rfloor - 2} \rfloor}, c_{\lfloor i/2^{\lfloor \log_2 i \rfloor - 1} \rfloor}, c_1$$

then there is some index for which the sequences differ. By β let us denote the first such index from the right. That is, $c_\beta \neq c'_\beta$, but $c_{\lfloor \beta/2 \rfloor} = c'_{\lfloor \beta/2 \rfloor}$ (at worst $\lfloor \beta/2 \rfloor = 1$). This means that the corresponding "messages" (1) for $i = \lfloor \beta/2 \rfloor$ are different, because $c_\beta \neq c'_\beta$, but the randomness used to make the signatures under the "messages" is the same, because $c_{\lfloor \beta/2 \rfloor} = c'_{\lfloor \beta/2 \rfloor}$. Assuming that Schnorr signatures are hard to repudiate this leads to leakage of signature keys.

See that due to hash value $H(\text{HS}_{i-1})$ present in "message" (1) the Stamp & Extend scheme may indeed be considered as a simple linear chain augmented with a mechanism providing logarithmic shortcuts to the root of the chain. The verification from Algorithm 4 (including line 8 of the Algorithm) executed for a given timestamp does not prove integrity of the whole data. It only shows that the timestamp checked must stand on the claimed position in the chain of timestamps, because the timestamp is anchored by a particular path (i.e., by a particular shortcut) to the certificate $Cert$. Of course, it witnesses that some parts of file HS are correct. Moreover, anybody can access the information from C and HS and check integrity of timestamps starting at any possible

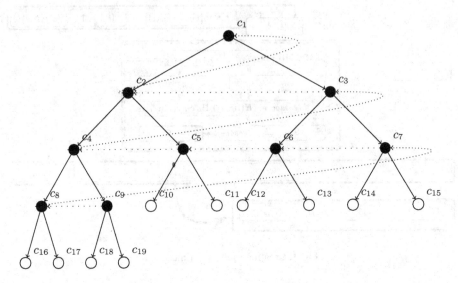

Fig. 2. The fuse of two structures (a chain and a binary tree) generated by consecutive calls of Algorithm 3 . The binary tree reflects dependencies between timestamps and commitments. The filled circles denote timestamps (and also the commitments already used), the empty circles are unused commitments. The dotted arrows denote hash links between consecutive timestamps in the chain.

Actors	: the requester or a third party
Input	: index i and access to the public lists C and HS
	or the sequence of records (2) and certificate $Cert$.
Output	: correct or incorrect with a proof of inconsistency

1 **begin**
2   check certificate $Cert$ and retrieve public key y from it
3   **for** $\alpha = 0, \ldots, \lfloor \log_2 i \rfloor$ **do**
4       $j := \lfloor i/2^\alpha \rfloor$
5   verify the signature $S_j = (e_j, s_j)$ under the corresponding "message" reconstructed from record (2) that includes S_j
6   check if the second element of the record (2) is indeed a hash of HS_{j-1}
7   reconstruct c_j by computing $c_j := g^{e_j} y^{s_j} h^{\ell_j}$
8   compare c_j with the jth element of C
9   **for** $j > 1$ check if c_j appears in the record (2) corresponding to $\alpha + 1$:
10   **case** if j is odd, then this should be the second element
11   if j is even, then this should be the first element
12   **for** $j = 1$ check if c_1 is confirmed by $Cert$

Algorithm 4: Verification of a timestamp.

location[1]. Even possibility of such an external audit (e.g., executed by competitors of TSA), should strongly discourage any misbehavior by TSA.

3 Security Analysis

3.1 External Adversaries $\mathcal{A}$

To facilitate security analysis let us first consider a restricted model of an external adversary (the restricted model shall be extended in Def. 3): Assume an adversary that attempts to create a timestamp matching one of the published commitments.

Definition 2. $\mathcal{A}_1$ *is given access to:*

- *list C of commitments (initially $C = [c_1]$),*
- *remaining data from HS (initially $\text{HS} = [Cert]$).*

$\mathcal{A}_1$ *can request TSA to issue some number of timestamps for hashes of $\mathcal{A}_1$'s choice. According to the number of requests (which is bounded by a polynomial in the security parameter $\kappa = \log_2 q$) both the list C and the file HS will grow.*

We assume that $\mathcal{A}_1$ wins, if he manages to issue a valid triple (S'_j, ℓ'_j, j), where S'_j is any[2] Schnorr signature being verified with TSA's public key y, corresponding to one of the unused commitments c_j.

Theorem 1. *In the standard model, the advantage of $\mathcal{A}_1$ is negligible, provided that solving DLP in $\langle g \rangle$ succeeds with a negligible probability.*

Proof. Let us assume that F_1 is an algorithm run by $\mathcal{A}_1$ that for n unused commitments enables him to deliver a valid triple (S'_j, ℓ'_j, j). Let $\delta_1^{(n)}$ denote success probability of F_1. Based on this we construct an algorithm (see Algorithm 5) that attempts to solve discrete logarithm problem for b, that is, to find a such that $b = g^a$.

Note that the assignment from line 12 for computing a follows from the equality $c_j = g^{s_j} y^{e_j} h^{\ell_j} = g^{s'_j} y^{e'_j} h^{\ell'_j}$. As ℓ_j is chosen at random, the condition from line 11 is false with probability $\frac{1}{q}$, thus Algorithm 5 returns a with probability $\delta_1^{(n)} \cdot (1 - \frac{1}{q})$. If breaking DLP has negligible success probability, then $\delta_1^{(n)} \cdot (1 - \frac{1}{q})$ must be negligible, too. As $1 - \frac{1}{q}$ is very close to 1, the value $\delta_1^{(n)}$ must be negligible, too. □

---

[1] For example, each requester receiving a timestamp (i.e., each client application) may always verify *a constant* number n_{ver} of timestamps: the one received and $n_{ver} - 1$ consecutive predecessors of a randomly chosen timestamp in the chain (the random choice is made by the requester). Moreover, we may assume that a local copy of all timestamps received is maintained by the requester, and a locally stored timestamp is compared with the newly received one if both are on the same position in the hash chain. Note that in case of misbehavior TSA may try to reduce probability of its detection by issuing an enormous number of timestamps for itself. However, this looks suspicious and may be the reason for thorough inspection of TSA.

[2] That is, we do not require that the message "signed" with S'_j has the form of a timestamp. Consequently, task of the adversary $\mathcal{A}_1$ does not become harder.

Input : a finite group generated by element g
an element $b \in \langle g \rangle$ for which discrete logarithm a is sought

Output : discrete logarithm a of b or $\bot$ in case of failure

1 **begin**
2   assign $h := b$
3   generate uniformly at random a "secret" key $x \in \{1, 2, \ldots, q-1\}$ of TSA and public key $y = g^x$
4   choose $k_1, \ell_1 \in \{0, 1, \ldots, q-1\}$ uniformly at random
5   generate $c_1 = g^{k_1} h^{\ell_1}$
6   run F_1
7   F_1 chooses some n bounded by a polynomial in κ: $n \leq Poly(\kappa)$
8   generate timestamps for H_i requested by F_1, $i = 1, \ldots, n$, (accordingly, file HS and list $C = [c_1, \ldots, c_{2n+1}]$ is made, where $c_i = g^{k_i} h^{\ell_i}$ for uniformly chosen $k_i, \ell_i \in \{0, 1, \ldots, q-1\}$, $i = 2, \ldots, 2n+1$)
9   with probability $\delta_1^{(n)}$ algorithm F_1 returns some valid triple (S'_j, ℓ'_j, j) where $j \in \{n+1, \ldots, 2n+1\}$, where $S'_j = (e'_j, s'_j)$ is *any* Schnorr signature being verified with TSA's public key y, signature made for message m'_j adaptively chosen by F_1
10   generate timestamps for $i = n+1, \ldots, 2n+1$ for H_i being hashes of random messages, as a result in the jth timestamp a triple (S_j, ℓ_j, j) is generated, where $S_j = (e_j, s_j)$
11   **if** $\ell_j \neq \ell'_j \bmod q$ **then**
12        $a := (s_j - s'_j + x(e_j - e'_j)) \cdot (\ell'_j - \ell_j)^{-1} \bmod q$
13   **return** a

14
15   **return** $\bot$

Algorithm 5: Breaking DLP with F_1.

Let us now extend the first model of external adversary: $\mathcal{A}_2$ is given access to the same data as $\mathcal{A}_1$, but is not restricted to utilize unused commitments only:

Definition 3. $\mathcal{A}_2$ *is given access to:*

- *list C of commitments (initially $C = [c_1]$),*
- *remaining data from* HS *(initially* HS $= [Cert]$).

$\mathcal{A}_2$ *can request TSA to issue some number of timestamps for hashes of $\mathcal{A}_2$'s choice.*

We assume that $\mathcal{A}_2$ wins, if he manages to issue a valid triple (S'_j, ℓ'_j, j), where S'_j is any Schnorr signature being verified with TSA's public key y, corresponding to any commitment c_j.

Theorem 2. *In the random oracle model, the advantage of $\mathcal{A}_2$ is negligible, provided that any adaptive chosen message attack aimed at private key of Schnorr signatures succeeds with a negligible probability.*

Proof (Sketch). Let us assume that F_2 is an algorithm run by $\mathcal{A}_2$ that for $2n+1$ commitments enables him to deliver a valid triple (S'_j, ℓ'_j, j). By

$$\delta_{eq,usd}^{(n)}, \delta_{neq,usd}^{(n)}, \delta_{eq,unsd}^{(n)}, \delta_{neq,unsd}^{(n)}$$

we denote the probabilities that F_2 succeeds respectively under the following conditions:

$$(\ell'_j = \ell_j) \wedge (1 \leq j \leq n),$$
$$(\ell'_j \neq \ell_j) \wedge (1 \leq j \leq n),$$
$$(\ell'_j = \ell_j) \wedge (n+1 \leq j \leq 2n+1),$$
$$(\ell'_j \neq \ell_j) \wedge (n+1 \leq j \leq 2n+1).$$

Let $\delta_2^{(n)} = \delta_{eq,usd}^{(n)} + \delta_{neq,usd}^{(n)} + \delta_{eq,unsd}^{(n)} + \delta_{neq,unsd}^{(n)}$.

On top of algorithm F_2 we build two algorithms, both incorporated into a single procedure (in fact the procedure defines the Challenger). On the very beginning of the resulting procedure a symmetric coin is tossed and according to toss result one of the two algorithms is executed. From F_2's point of view both algorithms are indistinguishable, that is, F_2 does not "know", what have called it. The coin toss shall introduce factor $\frac{1}{2}$ to reduction tightness.

We assume that F_2 can query q_H times random oracle $O_H(\cdot)$ for hash function H, and can query q_{sig} times random oracle $O_{sig,y}$, where $y \in \langle g \rangle$ is a public key for verification of signatures made by $O_{sig,y}$. Each of q_H, q_{sig} is bounded by some polynomial in a security parameter κ. Let len_H denote bit length of H.

We assume that all calls of the oracles made by F_2 shall be intercepted by the procedure mentioned above. The procedure shall compare arguments of the call with records of table T_H that were inserted by the second of the two algorithms, and if necessary a result from the appropriate table is returned to F_2.

The first of the two algorithms chosen by the coin toss works analogously to Algorithm 5: each occurrence of F_1 in Algorithm 5 should be replaced by F_2 and in line 9 of the algorithm $\delta_1^{(n)}$ should be replaced by $\delta_2^{(n)}$ and "$j \in \{n+1, \ldots, 2n+1\}$" by "$j \in \{1, \ldots, 2n+1\}$". Of course the modification is aimed at the event $\ell'_j \neq \ell_j$ which occurs with probability $\delta_{neq,usd}^{(n)} + \delta_{neq,unsd}^{(n)}$. Hence counting the coin toss, that is the probability that the algorithm resulting from the modification will fit the event, we get that the instance of DLP is solved with probability equal to $\frac{1}{2}(\delta_{neq,usd}^{(n)} + \delta_{neq,unsd}^{(n)})$. Therefore we get

$$\delta_{neq,usd}^{(n)} + \delta_{neq,unsd}^{(n)} \leq 2\epsilon^{(2n+1)}, \tag{3}$$

where $\epsilon^{(k)}$ is the upper bound for probability that DLP in group $\langle g \rangle$ may be broken with effort proportional to k.

The second algorithm is the Algorithm 6 . We shall argue that in the random oracle model its advantage differs negligibly from the advantage of an adaptive chosen message attack on private key of Schnorr signature scheme.

At the beginning of Algorithm 6 the target public key y is masked and randomized: $\tilde{y} := y \cdot g^{\tilde{x}}$. Thus, from F_2's point of view, the resulting public key $\tilde{y}$ of the time stamping service is uniformly distributed in $\langle g \rangle$. However, it is easy to convert the signatures obtained from the oracle $O_{sig,y}(\cdot)$ for public key y to signatures for public key $\tilde{y}$. It requires only "shifting" the second component of the signature (see the line 8).

Algorithm 6 makes commitments c_i in a different way than during the actual execution of Stamp&Extend. Namely, they are derived from signatures obtained from

---

Input : a finite group generated by element g
public key $y \in \langle g \rangle$ of Schnorr signatures
access to hashing oracle $O_H(\cdot)$ and to signing oracle $O_{sig,y}(\cdot)$

Output : discrete logarithm x of y or $\perp$ in case of failure

1 **begin**

2   choose $\tilde{x} \in \{0, 1, \ldots, q-1\}$ uniformly at random

3   set public key of the timestamping service as $\tilde{y} = y \cdot g^{\tilde{x}}$ /* masking y */

4   choose $h \in \langle g \rangle$ at random

5   set $\mathcal{MS} := \{0, \ldots, 2^{len_H} - 1\} \times \{0, \ldots, 2^{len_H} - 1\} \times \langle g \rangle \times \langle g \rangle \times \{0, \ldots, q-1\}$
    /* message space for the first 5 components of (1) */

6   choose $m_1 \in \{O_H(\mathrm{HS}_0)\} \times \{0, \ldots, 2^{len_H} - 1\} \times \langle g \rangle \times \langle g \rangle \times \{0, \ldots, q-1\} \times \{1\}$ with uniform probability distribution

7   call oracle $O_{sig,y}(\cdot)$ for m_1, let (e_1, s_1) be the signature returned for $O_{sig,y}(m_1)$

8   set $(\tilde{e_1}, \tilde{s_1}) := (e_1, s_1 - \tilde{x}e_1)$

9   assign $r_1 := g^{s_1} y^{e_1} (= g^{\tilde{s_1}} \tilde{y}^{\tilde{e_1}})$ and choose $\ell_1 \in \{0, 1, \ldots, q-1\}$ uniformly at random

10   put entry $(1, m_1 || r_1, \mathrm{NULL}, \tilde{e_1})$ to T_H and entry $(1, \tilde{e_1}, \tilde{s_1}, \ell_1)$ to T_{sig}

11   publish $c_1 = r_1 \cdot h^{\ell_1}$ as the first commitment on list C

12   run F_2

13   F_2 chooses some n bounded by a polynomial in κ: $n \leq Poly(\kappa)$

14   **for** *each timestamp request* H_i, $i = 1, \ldots, n$, *from* F_2 **do**

15   choose $m_{2i} \in \mathcal{MS} \times \{2i\}$, $m_{2i+1} \in \mathcal{MS} \times \{2i+1\}$ with uniform probability distribution

16   let (e_{2i}, s_{2i}) be result of $O_{sig,y}(m_{2i})$, (e_{2i+1}, s_{2i+1}) be result of $O_{sig,y}(m_{2i+1})$

17   set $(\tilde{e_{2i}}, \tilde{s_{2i}}) := (e_{2i}, s_{2i} - \tilde{x}e_{2i})$, $(\tilde{e_{2i+1}}, \tilde{s_{2i+1}}) := (e_{2i+1}, s_{2i+1} - \tilde{x}e_{2i+1})$

18   set $r_{2i} := g^{s_{2i}} \tilde{y}^{e_{2i}}$ and choose $\ell_{2i} \in \{0, 1, \ldots, q-1\}$ uniformly at random

19   put entry $(2i, m_{2i} || r_{2i}, \mathrm{NULL}, \tilde{e_{2i}})$ to T_H and entry $(2i, \tilde{e_{2i}}, \tilde{s_{2i}}, \ell_{2i})$ to T_{sig}

20   set $r_{2i+1} := g^{s_{2i+1}} \tilde{y}^{e_{2i+1}}$ and choose $\ell_{2i+1} \in \{0, 1, \ldots, q-1\}$ uniformly at random

21   put entry $(2i+1, m_{2i+1} || r_{2i+1}, \mathrm{NULL}, \tilde{e_{2i+1}})$ to T_H and entry $(2i+1, \tilde{e_{2i+1}}, \tilde{s_{2i+1}}, \ell_{2i+1})$ to T_{sig}

22   attach $c_{2i} = r_{2i} \cdot h^{\ell_{2i}}$ and $c_{2i+1} = r_{2i+1} \cdot h^{\ell_{2i+1}}$ to the public list C

23   set $\tilde{m_i} := (O_H(\mathrm{HS}_{i-1}), \mathrm{H}_i, c_{2i}, c_{2i+1}, \ell_i, i)$

24   **if** $O_H(\tilde{m_i} || r_i)$ *has been called by* F_2 *earlier and* $O_H(\tilde{m_i} || r_i) \neq \tilde{e_i}$ **then**

25   **return** $\perp$

26   replace $(i, m_i || r_i, \mathrm{NULL}, \tilde{e_i})$ in T_H with $(i, m_i || r_i, \tilde{m_i} || r_i, \tilde{e_i})$ /* hash replacement */

27   return to F_2: the record $\tilde{m_i}$ and the signature $(\tilde{e_i}, \tilde{s_i})$ read from T_{sig}

28   with probability $\delta_2^{(n)}$ algorithm F_2 returns some valid triple (S'_j, ℓ'_j, j), where $j \in \{1, \ldots, 2n+1\}$ and $S'_j = (e'_j, s'_j)$ is *any* Schnorr signature being verified with TSA's public key $\tilde{y}$; the Schnorr signature is made for message m'_j adaptively chosen by F_2

29   **if** $\ell_j = \ell'_j \bmod q$ *and* $\tilde{e_j} \neq e'_j \bmod q$ **then**

30         $x := (s'_j - \tilde{s_j}) \cdot (\tilde{e_j} - e'_j)^{-1} - \tilde{x} \bmod q$ /* based on
                                    $k_j = s'_j + (x + \tilde{x})e'_j = \tilde{s_j} + (x + \tilde{x})\tilde{e_j} \bmod q$ */

31

32   **return** x

33

34   **return** $\perp$

Algorithm 6: Breaking private key of Schnorr signatures with F_2.

oracle $O_{sig,y}(\cdot)$ for random messages. The random messages are chosen from domain corresponding to records (1) – set $\mathcal{MS}$ defined in line 5 of Algorithm 6 describes the first five coordinates of this message space, the last coordinate is message's index corresponding to the index of commitment currently made. The purpose of submitting random messages to the oracle is separation of the main operations during creation of Schnorr signatures by TSA. Namely, the value r is calculated *before* the message to be signed is presented by F_2. We have to keep in mind that the oracle $O_{sig,y}(\cdot)$ is a black box, and its operations are inseparable. So we cannot otherwise get the parameter $r = g^k$ which indirectly appears in the commitment $c = g^k h^l$.

At this point we take advantage of the random oracle model for the hash function H and of that the whole communication between F_2 and the oracles is intercepted by the main procedure defining the Challenger. Accordingly, the Challenger may cheat algorithm F_2 and return some values of its choice instead of the values that would be calculated by the oracles. In our case this happens with values returned for arguments $\widetilde{m}_i$ in line 23 of Algorithm 6 . That is, commitments are made on basis of signatures made for the random messages m_i, and then Algorithm 6 cheats algorithm F_2 that the signature that was created for m_i is in fact a fresh signature for $\widetilde{m}_i$, the signature that utilizes randomness r_i committed in c_i. To make the cheating successful the Challenger must intercept all future calls of $O_H(\cdot)$ for argument $\widetilde{m}_i \| r_i$ and return the answer $\widetilde{e}_i$, as it would be the answer of oracle $O_H(\cdot)$ called by the signature algorithm. Therefore Algorithm 6 makes at most n artificial collisions on H ("at most" because some of the collisions could also appear if the oracle $O_H(\cdot)$ would be used for the arguments).

The cheating would not be successful if at least one of the arguments $\widetilde{m}_i \| r_i$, $i = 1, \ldots, n$, was submitted by F_2 to the oracle $O_H(\cdot)$ before the argument was assembled by Algorithm 6 , and the result returned by $O_H(\cdot)$ was different than the result needed by Algorithm 6 (cf. condition in line 24). The cheating should be successful if F_2 would not detect any of the artificial collisions. Probability of finding some of the artificial collisions could be upper-bounded by probability of finding any collision on H. Note that F_2 knows at most $q_H + q_{sig} + 2n$ results of $H(\cdot)$ (indeed, q_{sig} hash values are due to signatures returned by the oracle $O_{sig,y}(\cdot)$ on F_2's requests, n results are returned by the Challenger as $O_H(\mathrm{HS}_{i-1})$, and n results are $\widetilde{e}_i = e_i$ which are also delivered by the Challenger). Being pretty conservative in estimating the upper bound for collision detection by F_2 for the purpose of this estimation we shall treat oracle $O_H(\cdot)$ just like a function (denoted as $H(\cdot)$). Let us count the values of $H(\cdot)$ that could be not used now because of the artificial collisions: in the worst case $\widetilde{m}_i \| r_i$ could have been the only argument yielding $H(\widetilde{m}_i \| r_i)$, in such a case replacing $H(\widetilde{m}_i \| r_i)$ with $H(m_i \| r_i)$, $i = 1, \ldots, n$, would limit results' space by at most n elements. Therefore the upper bound for collision detection by F_2 is $(q_H + q_{sig} + 2n) \cdot (q_H + q_{sig} + 2n - 1)/(2(2^{len_H} - n))$.

Since e_j, e'_j are both returned by the random oracle (value e'_j is always returned by $O_H(\cdot)$ when S'_j is being verified, and we have assumed that signature S'_j is valid), the event "$\widetilde{e}_j = e'_j \bmod q$" occurs with probability at most $2(q_H + q_{sig} + 2n - 1)/\min(q, 2^{len_H})$ (the coefficient "2" in the numerator results from the upper bound for maximum unbalance of distribution of results modulo q reduction, $2n - 1$ is the number of hash values obtained apart from $\widetilde{e}_j$ from the Challenger).

Finally, the attack is successful if Challenger's cheating is not detected and the condition in line 29 is satisfied. The probability of a successful attack is then at least:

$$(\delta_{eq,usd}^{(n)} + \delta_{eq,unsd}^{(n)}) \cdot \left(1 - \frac{(q_H + q_{sig} + 2n) \cdot (q_H + q_{sig} + 2n - 1)}{2(2^{len_H} - n)}\right) \cdot \left(1 - \frac{2(q_H + q_{sig} + 2n - 1)}{\min(q, 2^{len_H})}\right).$$

Counting the coin toss at the beginning of the main procedure the above expression should be multiplied with $\frac{1}{2}$.

Let $\epsilon_{Sch}^{(n)}$ be an upper bound for adversary's advantage in a chosen message attack on private key of Schnorr signature scheme, assuming the same adversary's effort is like in the algorithm above. Then:

$$\delta_{eq,usd}^{(n)} + \delta_{eq,unsd}^{(n)} \le 2\epsilon_{Sch}^{(n)} \cdot \left(1 - \frac{(q_H + q_{sig} + 2n) \cdot (q_H + q_{sig} + 2n - 1)}{2(2^{len_H} - n)}\right)^{-1} \cdot \left(1 - \frac{2(q_H + q_{sig} + 2n - 1)}{\min(q, 2^{len_H})}\right)^{-1}.$$

Since the attack on signature's private key is not harder than the attack on DLP defined in the same group of prime order (we have proved by the first of the two algorithms that the case "$\ell_j \ne \ell_j' \bmod q$" is negligibly close to DLP, cf. (3)) the theorem is proved.   □

3.2 Malicious TSA

Reusing Commitments. Subsect. 3.1 covers the case of an external attacker. Suppose now that TSA is going to issue two timestamps for different H_j, H_j' for the same commitment c_j. So what are the chances of malicious TSA to do it unnoticeably? The following theorem presents the key property of the scheme:

Theorem 3. *Assuming the standard model, a TSA re-using a commitment c_j for another timestamp would either find $\log_g h$ or would leak its own private key x or would break non-repudiation of Schnorr signature scheme.*

Proof (Sketch). Suppose we have two different timestamps for the same commitment c_j, made for different messages H_j, H_j' (cf. records (1)). Thereby we have two triples (e_j, s_j, ℓ_j), (e_j', s_j', ℓ_j'). If $\ell_j \ne \ell_j' \bmod q$, then $\log_g h$ is found by the TSA (compare lines 11-13 of Algorithm 5). Assume that $\ell_j = \ell_j' \bmod q$. If $e_j \ne e_j' \bmod q$, then the private key x leaks in the two timestamps (compare lines 29 and 32 of Algorithm 6, in present scenario $\tilde{x} = 0$). On the other hand, if $e_j = e_j' \bmod q$, then non-repudiation of Schnorr signatures is broken for the hash function inputs:

$$(H(HS_{j-1}), H_j, c_{2j}, c_{2j+1}, \ell_j, j)\|r_j \quad \text{and} \quad (H(HS_{j-1}), H_j', c_{2j}, c_{2j+1}, \ell_j, j)\|r_j$$

(note that $H_j \ne H_j'$, and due to re-usage of the commitment c_j and due to the assumption $\ell_j = \ell_j' \bmod q$ we get that r_j must be the same in both inputs, which is essential in breaking non-repudiation of Schnorr signatures).   □

Consequently, if $\log_g h$ is known to nobody and DLP in $\langle g \rangle$ is hard, and if Schnorr signatures are hard to repudiate, then making two timestamps for the same commitment would imply leak of the private exponent x of TSA.

Misbehavior Scenarios. In general, a malicious TSA may try the following tricks:

1. change a timestamp after issuing,
2. fork a chain of timestamps.
3. insert an additional timestamp in the past,
4. remove a timestamp.

Let us discuss each of these cases:

ad 1) this trick is covered by Theorem 3. Under the assumptions above the private key x must leak. Presenting the key x by a third party can be regarded in this case as a proof of breaking the scheme either by cryptanalysis or misbehavior of TSA – in both cases business of TSA should terminate.

ad 2) forking a chain at some place also requires creating two timestamps based on the same commitment, so the same remarks as above apply.

ad 3) inserting a timestamp is impossible since all places in the chain should be taken. Indeed, it is impossible to leave an empty space in the chain, since each timestamp is connected with the previous one and therefore such gaps must already have some fixed contents (even empty). Trying to reuse these places means delivering a new timestamp at a given point (see $H(\text{HS}_{i-1})$ in the record (1)). This leads to the same consequences as in the first case.

ad 4) removing a timestamp is impossible since, among others, the successor of a given timestamp is linked to it via a timestamp signature.

Rebuilding the Chain. Note that any third party that derives x can split the timestamp chain in the following way: assume that the timestamps are given for $t = 1, \ldots, 2m+1$. Then there are commitments for $t = 2m + 2, \ldots, 4m + 3$ as well, but the party does not attempt to open them. Note that the third party learns all exponents k_i for $i = 1, \ldots, 2m + 1$ from the equalities $s_i = k_i - xe_i \bmod q$. Therefore it can redo all steps from $m + 1$ through $2m + 1$, thereby issuing own commitments for all k_t for $t = 2m + 2, \ldots, 4m + 3$. Afterwards the third party can arbitrarily extend the chain.

Even if the security breach is evident (since given two chains arising from the same commitment anybody can derive secret key x, and may show the key as an evidence in court of justice), it is not clear which of the chains was the original one. Of course, the above attack requires redoing a large number of timestamps - so a large number of users would witnesses against a new chain. Additionally, this problem can be solved by the following countermeasure:

- from time to time TSA publishes a current timestamp in alternative way (in a newspaper),
- publishing a timestamp is compulsory when the index of the current timestamp is $2m + 1$ and the last published timestamp has index m.

It is easy to see that in this case a forged chain always halts before the next "anchor point" which is the published timestamp.

3.3 Long Term Security

Breaking signature scheme and/or leaking the signing key x of TSA brings some problems. However, as already observed above it means rather making mess than collapsing the current chain of signatures. Nevertheless, it seems to be reasonable to use the private key only for a limited period of time, and then, in order to prevent a future leakage, to destroy the key together with parameters (k, ℓ) used for Pedersen commitments. One can also demand that each timestamp must be confirmed with a digital signature by the requester immediately after receiving the timestamp. In this way one can speed up future disputes.

Note that if in the future the signature key is leaked or derived by some novel cryptanalytic method, this does not mean that an adversary will be able to misuse a Stamp & Extend service. Indeed, the second line of defense are the Pedersen commitments. The adversary will have either to get access to the parameters (k, ℓ) stored for future timestamps by TSA or to break DLP in order to provide arguments (k', ℓ') corresponding to the commitments.

4 Implementation Issues

Let us discuss key issues for scheme usability in practical scenario.

Instant Response. The main advantage of the scheme is that despite of efficient verification, the timestamp is returned immediately. This makes room for application of Stamp&Extend for instance by financial institutions, where the transactions have to be processed without delay.

Verification and Communication Complexity. The size of messages from requesters to TSA is constant, on the other hand the size of data necessary for complete verification of a timestamp with a serial number i is proportional to $\lfloor \log i \rfloor$, so in practice it is small enough. Moreover, TSA's computational effort for making the next timestamp is always constant.

Memory Usage. The scheme requires to hold the lists of timestamps and other auxiliary data. The lengths of these lists is bounded by $2i + 1$, where i is the number of timestamps issued so far.

If timestamping is intended to be a business service (and not for instance as a system log for a high speed system), then the number of timestamps and therefore the memory usage is a minor issue concerning contemporary technology and in no way is a bottleneck.

Necessity of Audits. In the classical scenario described by legal systems in many countries, time stamping requires a certified time-stamping devices, fulfilling some security profile. This process (apart from questionable value of such inspection for public) is costly not only due to the direct cost of examination, but also due to business risks concerning issuing certificates. If a security flaw is overlooked (which is quite likely in complicated cases), then the certification body can be sued and the height of compensation might be extreme.

A nice feature of Stamp&Extend system is that honesty of TSA can be forced without an external control. The only involvement of a third party is issuing the certificate $Cert$. However, this is a single certificate and the risk can be reduced by compulsory publishing the certificate in a non-electronic way (newspaper).

The audit of the chain of timestamps is done by the requesters. Of course, each requester makes only a small part of the job, but this makes it reasonable from business point of view: the requester does what is vital for his own interests.

Low-end Time Stamping. TSA might implement the service just on a PC and a reasonable (but cheap) device for issuing signatures and for exponentiations needed for commitments. The risk and responsibility for such a service can be defined accordingly. The upside of this solution is that security of the system has black-white nature: in case of a problem the system collapses in an undeniable way.

With many (academic) reservations against such solutions, one has to keep in mind that most systems successful in practice are not overshooting security requirements and work with quite modest security level.

Evidence in Case of Frauds. In case of a forgery made by TSA the evidence of fraud is undeniable in cryptographic sense. So there is no threat that a judge will deliver a judgment favorable for TSA even in a case when TSA is evidently guilty. This reduces to minimum the risk regarding lawsuits against malicious TSA.

5 Conclusions

We have presented a new timestamping scheme. Similarly like in [15] timestamp requests are served instantly. However, different security assumptions lead us to a centralized service with a setup phase reduced to generating a single commitment only. Moreover, security reductions for the protocol presented above are provided.

References

1. European Commision: Proposal for a regulation of the European Parliament and of the Council on electronic identification and trust services for electronic transactions in the internal market (June 4, 2012)
2. European Parliament and of the European Council: Directive 1999/93/ec of the European Parliament and of the Council of 13 December 1999 on a Community framework for electronic signatures. Official Journal of the European Communities L(13) (January 1, 2000)
3. Benaloh, J.C., de Mare, M.: Effcient broadcast time-stamping. Technical Report TR-MCS-91-1, Clarkson University Department of Mathematics and Computer Science (1991)
4. Haber, S., Stornetta, W.S.: How to time-stamp a digital document. J. Cryptology 3(2), 99–111 (1991)

5. Benaloh, J.C., de Mare, M.: One-Way Accumulators: A Decentralized Alternative to Digital Signatures (Extended Abstract). In: Helleseth, T. (ed.) EUROCRYPT 1993. LNCS, vol. 765, pp. 274–285. Springer, Heidelberg (1994)
6. Damgård, I., Mikkelsen, G.L.: Efficient, Robust and Constant-Round Distributed RSA Key Generation. In: Micciancio, D. (ed.) TCC 2010. LNCS, vol. 5978, pp. 183–200. Springer, Heidelberg (2010)
7. Le, D.P., Bonnecaze, A., Gabillon, A.: Signtiming scheme based on aggregate signature. In: ISI, pp. 145–149. IEEE (2008)
8. Buldas, A., Saarepera, M.: On Provably Secure Time-Stamping Schemes. In: Lee, P.J. (ed.) ASIACRYPT 2004. LNCS, vol. 3329, pp. 500–514. Springer, Heidelberg (2004)
9. Buldas, A., Laud, P., Saarepera, M., Willemson, J.: Universally Composable Time-Stamping Schemes with Audit. In: Zhou, J., López, J., Deng, R.H., Bao, F. (eds.) ISC 2005. LNCS, vol. 3650, pp. 359–373. Springer, Heidelberg (2005)
10. Buldas, A., Laur, S.: Do Broken Hash Functions Affect the Security of Time-Stamping Schemes? In: Zhou, J., Yung, M., Bao, F. (eds.) ACNS 2006. LNCS, vol. 3989, pp. 50–65. Springer, Heidelberg (2006)
11. Buldas, A., Niitsoo, M.: Can We Construct Unbounded Time-Stamping Schemes from Collision-Free Hash Functions? In: Baek, J., Bao, F., Chen, K., Lai, X. (eds.) ProvSec 2008. LNCS, vol. 5324, pp. 254–267. Springer, Heidelberg (2008)
12. Buldas, A., Niitsoo, M.: Optimally Tight Security Proofs for Hash-Then-Publish Time-Stamping. In: Steinfeld, R., Hawkes, P. (eds.) ACISP 2010. LNCS, vol. 6168, pp. 318–335. Springer, Heidelberg (2010)
13. Lipmaa, H.: On Optimal Hash Tree Traversal for Interval Time-Stamping. In: Chan, A.H., Gligor, V.D. (eds.) ISC 2002. LNCS, vol. 2433, pp. 357–371. Springer, Heidelberg (2002)
14. Blibech, K., Gabillon, A.: A New Timestamping Scheme Based on Skip Lists. In: Gavrilova, M.L., Gervasi, O., Kumar, V., Tan, C.J.K., Taniar, D., Laganá, A., Mun, Y., Choo, H. (eds.) ICCSA 2006. LNCS, vol. 3982, pp. 395–405. Springer, Heidelberg (2006)
15. Le, D.-P., Bonnecaze, A., Gabillon, A.: A Secure Round-Based Timestamping Scheme with Absolute Timestamps (Short Paper). In: Sekar, R., Pujari, A.K. (eds.) ICISS 2008. LNCS, vol. 5352, pp. 116–123. Springer, Heidelberg (2008)
16. Błaśkiewicz, P., Kubiak, P., Kutyłowski, M.: Two-Head Dragon Protocol: Preventing Cloning of Signature Keys - Work in Progress. In: Chen, L., Yung, M. (eds.) INTRUST 2010. LNCS, vol. 6802, pp. 173–188. Springer, Heidelberg (2011)
17. Schnorr, C.P.: Efficient signature generation by smart cards. J. Cryptology 4(3), 161–174 (1991)
18. BSI: Elliptic Curve Cryptography. Technische Richtlinie TR-03111 v2.0 (June 28, 2012)
19. Schnorr, C.: Method for identyfing subscribers and for generating and veryfing electronic signatures in a data exchange system. U.S. Patent 4,995,082 (1991)
20. Pedersen, T.P.: Non-interactive and Information-Theoretic Secure Verifiable Secret Sharing. In: Feigenbaum, J. (ed.) CRYPTO 1991. LNCS, vol. 576, pp. 129–140. Springer, Heidelberg (1992)
21. Kaliski Jr., B.S.: On Hash Function Firewalls in Signature Schemes. In: Preneel, B. (ed.) CT-RSA 2002. LNCS, vol. 2271, pp. 1–16. Springer, Heidelberg (2002)

Secure Implementation
of Asynchronous Method Calls and Futures

Peeter Laud

Cybernetica AS
peeter@cyber.ee

Abstract. Programming languages suitable for distributed computation contain constructs that should map well to the structure of the underlying system executing the programs, while being easily usable by the programmers and amenable to computer-aided verification. For object-oriented languages, *asynchronous method calls* returning *futures* that will be filled only after the called method has finished its execution have been proposed as a reasonably simple and analyzable programming construct. In this paper, we show how to map from a language with asynchronous method calls and futures to a language with explicit communication primitives and cryptographic operations. Our target language is reasonably similar to common process calculi, and translating it further to e.g. the applied pi calculus requires only known techniques. The translation is valid even for programs executing in *open* environments, where method calls and futures can be transmitted between the program and the environment.

Keywords: OO languages, process calculi, full abstraction.

1 Introduction

One of the main issues in the interplay of object-orientation and distribution in programming languages is the handling of method calls and returns between loosely coupled objects without losing the benefits of synchronization [27]. In this paper we are studying a language that proposes to strike a suitable balance between these issues. The *Abstract Behavioral Specification* (ABS) language [22,20] is an extension of Creol [23], currently used as the underlying formalism in a large-scale collaborative effort for formal verification of adaptable and evolvable software systems (http://hats-project.eu, [19]). The communication and synchronization abstractions of ABS have been carefully chosen to make the language convenient to use in modeling and specifying various concurrent systems [12,21], while at the same time supporting formal analysis and verification [11,28]. Thus the usage of ABS allows the design of *highly trusted* flexible software systems.

The inter-object messaging in ABS is based on asynchronous calls and futures. A method call immediately returns with a *future* that will be filled with the called method's result only after it has finished. At the same time, futures are first-class

C.J. Mitchell and A. Tomlinson (Eds.): INTRUST 2012, LNCS 7711, pp. 25–47, 2012.
© Springer-Verlag Berlin Heidelberg 2012

values and may be stored or passed around similarly to atomic data or object references. This makes possible very varied communication patterns between objects. At the source level, this communication is secured — the semantics of the language does not allow someone to intercept a message between two objects or to replace it with a different one.

The issues of actually securing the inter-object communication were likely not considered during the design of ABS. The advanced concepts in the construction of the language do not map well into the concepts of security systems and it is not clear at all how this communication should be protected in an actual distributed implementation. A *walled garden* approach could be taken if the whole program runs under a single authority; in this case, the communication between all objects is protected by a single key and appropriate cryptographic protocols can be used to prevent replays by the adversary. If the program is *open* — different objects are controlled by different, mutually distrustful authorities — then this approach no longer works as long as calls between different authorities as possible.

In this paper we show how the communication between objects in ABS can be protected using cryptographic techniques. We propose a *fully abstract* translation from the ABS language to a language with explicit message-passing and cryptographic operations — two programs in ABS are indistinguishable iff their translations are indistinguishable. Hence this translation preserves all observable properties of programs, including all different kinds of security properties (integrity, secrecy, non-interference, etc.). In this paper, we are considering the symbolic semantics of cryptographic operations (perfect cryptography, or Dolev-Yao model) [15]. For computational soundness, the results of [13] may be applicable if encryption cycles are avoided. We believe that our implementation language can be straightforwardly translated into well-known process calculi, e.g. the applied pi calculus, such that a program in our implementation language and its translation are observationally equivalent. Besides being an interesting result in characterizing which communication models can be fully abstracted using cryptography (we discuss this more in the next section), our result also allows to carry over the verification results obtained for the ABS language to its implementation and thus serves as a validation of the design of ABS.

2 Related Work

There has been a fair amount of work in securely translating the abstractions of communication back into the exchanging of messages on point-to-point channels between entities. This line of work was started by Abadi et al. [3,4] who show how channels protected by the knowledge of names can be securely implemented using public channels where the messages are protected through cryptographic means. The translation is applied to processes specified in the join-calculus [16]; its restrictive scope extrusion rules help to simplify the translation. The source language is abstracted further by introducing authentication primitives in [5]. Authentication primitives in a π-calculus setting have been considered by Backes et al. [8]. Securing the channels with cryptographic mechanisms has also been explored by Bugliesi and Focardi [9], and by Mödersheim and Viganó [26] who consider languages containing confidential and/or authentic channels between principals and ways to simulate them on unprotected channels using cryptography. Adão and Fournet [7] consider the translation of authentic channels between principals directly into channels protected by cryptography in the *computational* model [18]. Bugliesi and Giunti [10] give a translation for a variation of π-calculus with normal scope extrusion rules, but with capability types on channel names and a proxy service in the translated process that has no counterpart in the original.

Abstract information protection primitives and their implementation has also been considered in the language-based information flow security community. Vaughan and Zdancewic [31] consider the *packing/unpacking* of information at certain level of the information flow lattice; code executing with lower privileges cannot access high-packed data. Fournet and Rezk [17] consider programs with holes for adversary's code; the program data must be protected across these holes.

Abadi [1] has discussed the role full abstraction plays in the implementations of secure systems, as well as the difficulties in achieving it. He notes that for the full π-calculus, the unconstrained distribution of read-capabilities of channels, together with the requirement of forward secrecy (messages exchanged on a channel before the adversary obtained the read-capability for that channel remain secret) makes fully abstract translations to cryptographically protected channels hard to construct. On the other hand, in the join-calculus [3,4] only write-capabilities can be distributed.

The constructs of ABS give rise to two different kinds of channels. An object reference can be used to send messages (invoke methods) to that object. This represents a channel where the write-capability can be freely distributed, but the read-capability is only at the object. This channel is similar to the channels of join-calculus. A future represents a channel where the read-capability can be freely distributed, but the write-capability is owned by a single task. According to π-calculus semantics, such channel would pose difficulties for a fully abstract translation, but the semantics of ABS makes it possible by not requiring forward secrecy. The handshake that takes place during a method invocation is possibly the trickiest feature to translate. Here a message on the first kind of channel causes the creation of a second kind of channel, such that the recipient has the write- and the sender the read-capability. A method invocation is atomic in ABS, hence the translation must be atomic, too.

3   The Source Language

3.1   Syntax

Our source language is a simplified version of (the object-oriented fragment of) ABS, retaining all the interesting details of inter-object communication and parallelism. We leave out the semaphore-based cooperative synchronization of tasks belonging to the same object, as our translation is orthogonal to those and

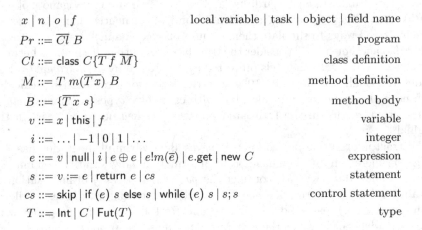

Fig. 1. Syntax of the source language

it is well-known how to express semaphores in π-calculus [25]. The (abstract) syntax of the source language is given in Figure 1. The notation $\overline{X}$ denotes a sequence of X-s.

Let us explain the language constructs related to parallel distributed execution. Each object executes independently of others (i.e. the objects are the grains of distribution), the objects communicate *only* by asynchronous method calls (e.g. it is impossible to directly read or write some field of some object from inside another object). Each object belongs to some class; different classes have different methods. Each object may concurrently execute a number of tasks. In ABS, the scheduling of tasks belonging to the same object, is cooperative [20]. For simplifying the presentation in this paper, we let the tasks also execute independently of each other (the next task to make a step is chosen nondeterministically from the set of all tasks). The names of objects and tasks are picked from a countable set **N**.

The expression $e!m(\overline{e})$ denotes the *asynchronous* call of the method m. The call immediately returns a future. At the same time, a new task executing the code of m is started at the receiver of the call. The get-construct is used to read the value of that future, if it is available. If not, then **get** blocks. The expression $e \oplus e$ denotes the application of any binary operation to two expressions. In the actual implementations, there may be several different operations. In particular, $\oplus$ may denote the comparison of two values.

As specified in Fig. 1, the language does not contain means to prevent type errors. We assume that reasonable default values are used whenever a type error is detected at runtime (0 for integers, null for object references, a never-available future for futures, including the results of method calls on null).

3.2   Operational Semantics

The semantics of a program Pr is a labeled transition system (LTS). In general, a LTS is a quadruple $\mathcal{L} = (S, A, \rightarrow, s_0)$, where S is the set of *states*, A is the set of *labels* (both can be infinite), $\rightarrow$ is a subset of $S \times A \times S$, and $s_0 \in S$ is the starting state. We write $s \xrightarrow{\alpha} s'$ for $(s, \alpha, s') \in \rightarrow$. We assume that A contains a special label τ that we call the *silent label*. A LTS communicates with its outside environment through its transitions that carry non-silent labels.

The semantics $[\![Pr]\!]$ of ABS programs (as closed systems) is given in [20]. The semantics of a program as a closed system can be seen as a LTS where all transitions are labeled τ. An open-system semantics of an ABS-like language is considered in [6] and our treatment is a simplified version of that.

A *run-time* configuration —the state of the LTS— of a program is a set of objects. Each object is related to zero or more tasks. The configuration also records object and task names that are made known to the environment. Formally, the run-time configurations are as follows:

$$P ::= o[C, \sigma, \varphi] \mid n \langle o, \sigma, s \rangle \mid \mathsf{p}(o) \mid \mathsf{p}(n) \mid P \parallel P$$

Each object is represented by its identifier o, its class C, its state σ (the values of its fields), and the values of the futures it has received φ (a mapping from names to values). Each task is represented by its identifier n, its object o, the statement s that is yet to be executed in this task, and its state σ (the values of its local variables). Both o and n are *names*. The names of objects and tasks do not repeat inside a configuration. The operation $\parallel$ is considered to be commutative and associative.

The notation $\mathsf{p}(o)$ means that the name o is *public* — the environment knows it. It is possible for an environment to know the name o without the object $o[C, \sigma, \varphi]$ being part of the configuration. This means that the environment controls and executes that object. The notation $\mathsf{p}(n)$ means the same for task names n. For a configuration P, let $\mathcal{N}(P)$ denote all object and task names in the configuration. Let $\mathcal{N}_\mathsf{p}(P)$ and $\mathcal{N}_\mathsf{l}(P)$ denote all public names in P, and all local names in P (i.e. names of objects and tasks present in P), respectively.

The evaluation contexts for expressions and statements are defined as follows. We let c range over the *constants* — integers, null, and names. The hole $[]$ will be filled with the expression that will be evaluated during the next computation step.

$$e^{[]} ::= [] \mid e^{[]} \oplus e \mid c \oplus e^{[]} \mid e^{[]}!m(\overline{e}) \mid c!m(\overline{c}, e^{[]}, \overline{e}) \mid e^{[]}.\mathsf{get}$$
$$s^{[]} ::= v := e^{[]} \mid \mathsf{return}\ e^{[]} \mid \mathsf{if}\ (e^{[]})\ s\ \mathsf{else}\ s \mid \mathsf{while}\ (e^{[]})\ s \mid s^{[]}; s$$

The transition rules of the LTS $[\![Pr]\!]$ are given in Fig. 2. In these rules we make the following convention: if a task $n\langle o, \ldots \rangle$ is part of a configuration, then the object $o[\ldots]$ is also a part of it, even if it is not shown.

In the semantics, the rule (acall_1) describes a method call from an object o to o', both in the configuration. A new task is created which starts in a suspended state. The call immediately returns a future whose value is equal to the name of

$$\frac{}{n\langle o,\sigma,s[x]\rangle \xrightarrow{\tau} n\langle o,\sigma,s[\sigma(x)]\rangle} \ \text{(rv)} \qquad \frac{}{n\langle o,\sigma,x:=c\rangle \xrightarrow{\tau} n\langle o,\sigma[x\mapsto c],\text{skip}\rangle} \ \text{(wv)}$$

$$\frac{}{o[C,\sigma,\varphi] \parallel n\langle o,\sigma',s[f]\rangle \xrightarrow{\tau} o[C,\sigma,\varphi] \parallel n\langle o,\sigma',s[\sigma(f)]\rangle} \ \text{(rf)}$$

$$\frac{}{o[C,\sigma,\varphi] \parallel n\langle o,\sigma',f:=c\rangle \xrightarrow{\tau} o[C,\sigma[f\mapsto c],\varphi] \parallel n\langle o,\sigma',\text{skip}\rangle} \ \text{(wf)}$$

$$\frac{}{n\langle o,\sigma,s[c_1\oplus c_2]\rangle \xrightarrow{\tau} n\langle o,\sigma,s[[\![\oplus]\!](c_1,c_2)]\rangle} \ \text{(arith)}$$

$$\frac{}{n\langle o,\sigma,\text{skip};s\rangle \xrightarrow{\tau} n\langle o,\sigma,s\rangle} \ \text{(skip)} \qquad \frac{n\langle o,\sigma,s_1\rangle \xrightarrow{\tau} n\langle o,\sigma,s_1'\rangle}{n\langle o,\sigma,s_1;s_2\rangle \xrightarrow{\tau} n\langle o,\sigma,s_1';s_2\rangle} \ \text{(seq)}$$

$$\frac{c\neq 0}{n\langle o,\sigma,\text{if }(c)\ s_1\text{ else }s_2\rangle \xrightarrow{\tau} n\langle o,\sigma,s_1\rangle} \ \text{(if}_1\text{)} \qquad \frac{}{n\langle o,\sigma,\text{if }(0)\ s_1\text{ else }s_2\rangle \xrightarrow{\tau} n\langle o,\sigma,s_2\rangle} \ \text{(if}_2\text{)}$$

$$\frac{c\neq 0}{n\langle o,\sigma,\text{while }(c)\ s\rangle \xrightarrow{\tau} n\langle o,\sigma,s;\text{while }(c)\ s\rangle} \ \text{(while}_1\text{)}$$

$$\frac{}{n\langle o,\sigma,\text{while }(0)\ s\rangle \xrightarrow{\tau} n\langle o,\sigma,\text{skip}\rangle} \ \text{(while}_2\text{)}$$

$$\frac{\text{body}(m)=s \qquad s_{task}=s[\bar{c}/params(m)] \qquad n'\neq n}{o'[\ldots] \parallel n\langle o,\sigma,s[o'!m(\bar{c})]\rangle \xrightarrow{o\to o'} o'[\ldots] \parallel n\langle o,\sigma,s[n']\rangle \parallel n'\langle o',\sigma_{init},s_{task}\rangle \parallel \mathsf{p}(o) \parallel \mathsf{p}(o')} \ \text{(acall}_1\text{)}$$

$$\frac{o'\neq o \qquad names(\bar{c})=\{c_1,\ldots,c_k\} \qquad n'\notin\{n,c_1,\ldots,c_k\}}{n\langle o,\sigma,s[o'!m(\bar{c})]\rangle \parallel \mathsf{p}(o') \xrightarrow{o\to n'[o'.m(\bar{c})]} n\langle o,\sigma,s[n']\rangle \parallel \mathsf{p}(o') \parallel \mathsf{p}(o) \parallel \mathsf{p}(c_1) \parallel \cdots \parallel \mathsf{p}(c_k)} \ \text{(acall}_2\text{)}$$

$$\frac{n\notin names(\bar{c})=\{c_1,\ldots,c_k\} \qquad \text{body}(m)=s \qquad s_{task}=s[\bar{c}/params(m)]}{o[\ldots] \parallel \mathsf{p}(o) \parallel \mathsf{p}(c_1) \parallel \cdots \parallel \mathsf{p}(c_k) \xrightarrow{n=o!m(\bar{c})} o[\ldots] \parallel \mathsf{p}(o) \parallel \mathsf{p}(c_1) \parallel \cdots \parallel \mathsf{p}(c_k) \parallel \mathsf{p}(n) \parallel n\langle o,\sigma_{init},s_{task}\rangle} \ \text{(acall}_3\text{)}$$

$$\frac{\varphi(n')\text{ is undefined}}{o[C,\sigma,\varphi] \parallel n'\langle o',\sigma',\text{return }c;s\rangle \xrightarrow{o\leftarrow o'} o[l,C,\varphi[n'\mapsto c]] \parallel n'\langle o',\sigma',\text{return }c;s\rangle \parallel \mathsf{p}(o) \parallel \mathsf{p}(o')} \ \text{(return}_1\text{)}$$

$$\frac{}{\mathsf{p}(n) \parallel n\langle o,\sigma,\text{return }c;s\rangle \xrightarrow{n[c]\leftarrow o} \mathsf{p}(n) \parallel n\langle o,\sigma,\text{return }c;s\rangle \parallel \mathsf{p}(o) \parallel \mathsf{p}(names(c))} \ \text{(return}_2\text{)}$$

$$\frac{n\neq n' \qquad \varphi(n')\text{ is undefined}}{o[C,\sigma,\varphi] \parallel \mathsf{p}(n') \parallel \mathsf{p}(names(c)) \xrightarrow{o\leftarrow n'[c]} o[C,\sigma,\varphi[n'\mapsto c]] \parallel \mathsf{p}(n') \parallel \mathsf{p}(o) \parallel \mathsf{p}(names(c))} \ \text{(return}_3\text{)}$$

$$\frac{\varphi(n')\text{ is defined}}{o[C,\sigma,\varphi] \parallel n\langle o,\sigma',s[n'.\text{get}]\rangle \xrightarrow{\tau} o[C,\sigma,\varphi] \parallel n\langle o,\sigma',s[\varphi(n')]\rangle} \ \text{(get)}$$

$$\frac{}{\square \xrightarrow{\nu n} \mathsf{p}(n)} \ \text{(newn)} \qquad \frac{o'\neq o}{n\langle o,\sigma,s[\text{new }C]\rangle \xrightarrow{\tau} n\langle o,\sigma,s[o']\rangle \parallel o'[C,\sigma_{init},\varphi_{empty}]} \ \text{(newc)}$$

$$\frac{}{\square \xrightarrow{\nu o} \mathsf{p}(o)} \ \text{(newo)} \qquad \frac{P\xrightarrow{\alpha}P' \qquad \mathcal{N}_{\text{f}}(\alpha)\cap\mathcal{N}_{\text{l}}(P'')=\emptyset}{P\parallel P'' \xrightarrow{\alpha} P'\parallel P''} \ \text{(frame)}$$

Fig. 2. Operational semantics of the source language

the new task. This call is visible to the environment (o made a method call to o'), but called method and its arguments are supposed to be protected. The names o and o' both become known to the environment, too. This is our design choice, because protecting against eavesdropping is supposedly cheap, but protecting against traffic analysis is expensive. The rule (acall$_2$) describes a method call from an object o in the configuration to an object o' in the environment. In this case, the environment learns the caller, as well as all arguments of the method. The rule (acall$_3$) describes a call from the environment to an object in the configuration. A name can be among the arguments of the call only if it is already known to the environment. There is no constraint on the integer arguments.

The rules (return$_i$) describe the returning of the result of a completed task. If the object receiving the value belongs to the configuration, it saves the returned value in its φ-component. Later, the get-expression may read it from φ; this is no longer visible to the environment. We have made a design choice that the result of a completed task may be returned to an object at most once. Most importantly, this means that all expressions n.get in the tasks of some object o return the same value. In a different object o', the value of n.get may be different (if n is the name of a task managed by the environment). In an implementation, it is simple to ensure the uniqueness of returned values in a single object, while comparing them across all objects requires complex protocols, e.g. Byzantine agreement.

Rule (newc) describes the creation of a new object. The creation is invisible to the environment, which does not learn the name of the new object. This allows the new object to be initialized by its creator (the first method call to the newly created object must necessarily come from the program, not from the environment, unless the program chooses to leak the identity of the newly generated object before placing any calls). This also allows the identities of objects to serve as passwords (that the adversary does not know). So the programmer can control how much interaction with the environment is allowed/possible.

The environment can also generate new names for objects and tasks (rules (newn) and (newo)); $\square$ denotes the empty environment (unit element for $\parallel$). Finally, the (frame) rule states that each of the steps can also occur in a larger context, if the context does not interfere with the step. The set $\mathcal{N}_f(\alpha)$ denotes all names in α that cannot be local names in a configuration to which a transition labeled by α is made. It is defined by

$$\mathcal{N}_f(o \rightarrow n'[o'.m(\overline{c})]) = \{o', n'\} \qquad \mathcal{N}_f(\nu n) = \{n\}$$
$$\mathcal{N}_f(o \leftarrow n'[c]) = \{n'\} \qquad \mathcal{N}_f(\nu o) = \{o\} \ .$$

For other labels, $\mathcal{N}_f(\alpha) = \emptyset$. Also, when writing $P' \parallel P''$, we assume the objects and tasks in P' and P'' have different names.

The initial configuration for the program $Cl \ \{\overline{T\,x}\ s\}$ will consist of just the task $n_0 \langle \text{null}, \sigma, s \rangle$. This task is the only task that is not tied to an object (all tasks created later will be tied to some object).

We denote the set of all labels occurring in Fig. 2 by Act_{src}.

4   The Implementation Language

We now present our implementation language. Its main differences from the source language are

- explicit message passing replaces asynchronous method calls;
- the spawning of new tasks is decided locally;
- cryptographic techniques, not the knowledge of names is used to protect the communication between objects;
- objects and tasks do not have names, but are identified through their keys.

As such, the communication primitives of our implementation language are the same as in well-known cryptographic process calculi, e.g. the applied pi-calculus [2]. We retain the syntactic constructions for classes, methods, and program state from our source language. It is known how to translate these constructions into the π-calculus [24,29]. Thus we believe that we are justified in considering our implementation language as a dialect of the applied pi-calculus.

4.1   Syntax

Our implementation language contains cryptographic operations for the construction of messages exchanged between objects. The exact set of available operations does (mostly) not affect the syntax or semantics of the language, hence we defer its specification to Sec. 5 where we explain how to translate from the source to the implementation language. We assume we are given a signature Σ containing possible operations together with their arities. Also, there is an equational theory over cryptographic messages that specifies the cancellation and other rules. We let F range over the operations in Σ. For each $F \in \Sigma$, there will be an an operation that can be invoked in expressions; this operation applies F to its arguments. By overloading the notation, we let F denote that operation as well (hence the rule (crypt) in Fig. 4).

Still, there are a couple of operations that we need Σ to contain. As we want to identify the objects by their public keys, we require Σ to contain unary operations $\cdot^+$ and $\cdot^-$. No cancellation rules are associated with just these operations.

The syntax of the implementation language is given in Fig. 3. Compared to the source language, the first difference that we spot is the extra method body — the "main method" — in the class declarations. We denote the main method of a class C by $C.run$. This method is executed immediately after an object has been created and it will remain active for the entire lifetime of the object. Another difference is, that we require each class to have fields k_{pub} and k_{priv} where the public and private key of a newly generated object are saved upon its creation.

The expressions $e!m(\bar{e})$ for method calls and $e.get$ for reading the value of a future have disappeared from the language. Instead, there is a statement $\text{send}(e_1, e_2)$ that sends the message e_2 to the object with the public key e_1. There is also an expression recv that returns a message that has been sent to this object. Note that messages are sent to objects, not tasks.

$$
\begin{array}{llr}
x \mid a \mid f & & \text{local variable} \mid \text{atom} \mid \text{field name} \\
Pr ::= \overline{Cl}\ B & & \text{program} \\
Cl ::= \text{class } C\{\overline{T\,f}\ \overline{M}\ B\} & & \text{class definition} \\
M ::= T\ m(\overline{T\,x})\ B & & \text{method definition} \\
B ::= \{\overline{T\,x}\ s\} & & \text{method body} \\
v ::= x \mid \text{this} \mid f & & \text{variable} \\
i ::= \ldots \mid -1 \mid 0 \mid 1 \mid \ldots & & \text{integer} \\
e ::= v \mid \text{null} \mid i \mid e \oplus e \mid a \mid F(e,\ldots,e) & & \\
\quad \mid \text{new } C \mid \text{recv} \mid \text{newatom} \mid \text{unbox}(e) & & \text{expression} \\
s ::= v := e \mid \text{send}(e,e) \mid \text{spawn } m(\overline{e}) \mid cs & & \text{statement} \\
cs ::= \text{skip} \mid \text{if } (e)\ s \text{ else } s \mid \text{while } (e)\ s \mid s;s & & \text{control statement} \\
T ::= \text{Int} \mid \text{Msg} & & \text{type}
\end{array}
$$

Fig. 3. Syntax of the implementation language

The expression newatom picks a new atomic cryptographic message (usable as a nonce, key, etc.) from a countable set $\mathcal{A}$. The expression $F(e_1,\ldots,e_n)$ constructs a new cryptographic message by applying the constructor F to the messages $e_1,\ldots,e_n$. The argument e_i may also be an integer; in this case, it will automatically be boxed as a message. For the opposite conversion, there is an explicit operation unbox (returns 0 if the argument is not a boxed integer). Again we assume the existence of a reasonable type system that avoids the mixing up of values of type Int and Msg. Besides these two types, our implementation language may reasonably include values of other types, and our translation procedure given in the next section will indeed need more types. These types do not affect the translatability of our implementation language into the applied pi calculus.

Finally, the spawn-statement is used to spawn new tasks. It adds a new task *at the same object* where the spawn-statement was executed. This task will execute the body of the method m. Note that spawn is a statement, not an expression. Hence it does not return anything.

4.2 Operational Semantics

In the implementation language, object and future names are replaced by cryptographic messages. In particular, each object is represented by its public key and each task is identified by an atom. The set of values c is now generated by the grammar

$$
c ::= i \mid a \mid \text{null} \mid F(c,\ldots,c)\ .
$$

Here null has the type Msg. We may also denote a value by E if we want to stress that it is a cryptographic message. We can also use the notation $E(x_1,\ldots,x_l)$ which denotes a message containing the variables $x_1,\ldots,x_l$; such message becomes a value if these variables are substituted with values.

The semantics of a program Pr in the implementation language is again a LTS, albeit with a different set of labels. Its runtime configurations are given by the grammar

$$P ::= k^+[C,\sigma] \mid \langle k^+, \sigma, s \rangle \mid \mathsf{g}(a) \mid \mathsf{p}(x\backslash E) \mid P \parallel P \ .$$

Here $k^+[C,\sigma]$ is an object of class C with the public key k^+ and values of fields σ. A task $\langle k^+, \sigma, s \rangle$ of this object k^+ does not have a name, but it has the values of local variables σ and the yet-to-be-executed statement s. The runtime configuration $\mathsf{g}(a)$ records that an atomic message a has been generated. The configuration $\mathsf{p}(x\backslash E)$ records that the environment has learned the message E built from atomic messages (and integers) using the constructors in Σ, and this message is available to the environment through the variable x, picked from a countable set $\mathcal{X}$. The components $\mathsf{p}(x\backslash E)$ are similar to the *frame* of a process in the applied pi calculus. The transitions ensure that the environment of the program can only perform operations that are consistent with the model of symbolic cryptography.

Let $\mathsf{NV}(P)$ denote the set of all names and variables *defined* in the configuration. If $u \in \mathcal{A} \cup \mathcal{X}$ then $u \in \mathsf{NV}(P)$ iff $u^+[\ldots]$, $\mathsf{g}(u)$, or $\mathsf{p}(u\backslash E)$ belongs to P.

The transitions of the LTS $[\![Pr]\!]$ are given in Fig. 4. Similarly to the presentation of the semantics of the source language in Fig. 2, we use the convention that if a task $\langle K, \ldots \rangle$ is mentioned in the configuration, then the object $K[\ldots]$ is also a part of that configuration, even if it has been omitted from the rule.

The rule (send$_1$) describes the transmission of messages from one object in the configuration to another one. The first argument of send is the identity (the public key) of the receiver. If it equals null then anyone (including the adversary) may receive that message. Importantly, the sender will not proceed before the receiver has received the message. This is similar to the method call in the source language where, after making the call, the caller knows that the callee has received it. The adversary sees the identity of the sender, the identity of the receiver, and the message. All these are bound to new variables $k_1, k_2, x \in \mathcal{X}$ that the adversary may use afterwards. The rule (send$_2$) describes the transmission of a message where the sender is in the configuration, but the receiver is not. The adversary gets exactly the same information. If the receiver of the message is specified as null then both rules are applicable.

The rule (send$_3$) describes the reception of a message sent by the adversary. It is an example of how the adversary can use the messages it has received. Namely, the adversary specifies a message with variables $x_1, \ldots, x_l \in \mathcal{X}$ that are bound to values $c_1, \ldots, c_l$ in the configuration. These values will be substituted in place of the variables in the received message. This construction allows the adversary to specify precisely those messages that it can construct from the received messages according to the rules of symbolic cryptography.

The rule (crypt) handles the application of cryptographic constructors and the rule (unbox) the unboxing of integers. The function *unbox* returns i if its argument was a boxed integer i, and 0 otherwise. The rules (newa) and (newn)

$$\frac{}{\langle K,\sigma, s[x]\rangle \xrightarrow{\tau} \langle K,\sigma, s[\sigma(x)]\rangle}\ (\mathrm{rv}')\qquad\qquad \frac{}{\langle K,\sigma, x := c\rangle \xrightarrow{\tau} \langle K,\sigma[x \mapsto c], \mathsf{skip}\rangle}\ (\mathrm{wv}')$$

$$\frac{}{K[C,\sigma]\ \|\ \langle K,\sigma', s[f]\rangle \xrightarrow{\tau} K[C,\sigma]\ \|\ \langle K,\sigma', s[\sigma(f)]\rangle}\ (\mathrm{rf}')$$

$$\frac{}{K[C,\sigma]\ \|\ \langle K,\sigma', f := c\rangle \xrightarrow{\tau} K[C,\sigma[f \mapsto c]]\ \|\ \langle K,\sigma', \mathsf{skip}\rangle}\ (\mathrm{wf}')$$

$$\frac{}{\langle K,\sigma, s[c_1 \oplus c_2]\rangle \xrightarrow{\tau} \langle K,\sigma, s[[\![\oplus]\!](c_1, c_2)]\rangle}\ (\mathrm{arith}')$$

$$\frac{}{\langle K,\sigma, \mathsf{skip}; s\rangle \xrightarrow{\tau} \langle K,\sigma, s\rangle}\ (\mathrm{skip}')\qquad \frac{\langle K,\sigma, s_1\rangle \xrightarrow{\tau} \langle K,\sigma, s_1'\rangle}{\langle K,\sigma, s_1; s_2\rangle \xrightarrow{\tau} \langle K,\sigma, s_1'; s_2\rangle}\ (\mathrm{seq}')$$

$$\frac{c \neq 0}{\langle K,\sigma, \mathsf{if}\ (c)\ s_1\ \mathsf{else}\ s_2\rangle \xrightarrow{\tau} \langle K,\sigma, s_1\rangle}\ (\mathrm{if}_1')\qquad \frac{}{\langle K,\sigma, \mathsf{if}\ (0)\ s_1\ \mathsf{else}\ s_2\rangle \xrightarrow{\tau} \langle K,\sigma, s_2\rangle}\ (\mathrm{if}_2')$$

$$\frac{c \neq 0}{\langle K,\sigma, \mathsf{while}\ (c)\ s\rangle \xrightarrow{\tau} \langle K,\sigma, s; \mathsf{while}\ (c)\ s\rangle}\ (\mathrm{while}_1')$$

$$\frac{}{\langle K,\sigma, \mathsf{while}\ (0)\ s\rangle \xrightarrow{\tau} \langle K,\sigma, \mathsf{skip}\rangle}\ (\mathrm{while}_2')$$

$$\frac{K_2' = K_2 \vee K_2' = \mathsf{null}}{\langle K_1,\sigma, \mathsf{send}(K_2',c); s\rangle\ \|\ \langle K_2,\sigma', s'[\mathsf{recv}]\rangle \xrightarrow{k_1 \to k_2 : x}}\ (\mathrm{send}_1)$$
$$\langle K_1,\sigma, s\rangle\ \|\ \langle K_2,\sigma', s'[c]\rangle\ \|\ \mathsf{p}(x\backslash c)\ \|\ \mathsf{p}(k_1\backslash K_1)\ \|\ \mathsf{p}(k_2\backslash K_2)$$

$$\frac{K_2 \neq K_1}{\langle K_1,\sigma, \mathsf{send}(K_2,c); s\rangle \xrightarrow{k_1 \to k_2 : x} \langle K_1,\sigma, s\rangle\ \|\ \mathsf{p}(x\backslash c)\ \|\ \mathsf{p}(k_1\backslash K_1)\ \|\ \mathsf{p}(k_2\backslash K_2)}\ (\mathrm{send}_2)$$

$$\frac{K_2 \neq K_1 \qquad \forall x_i : \theta(x_i) = c_i}{\langle K_2,\sigma', s'[\mathsf{recv}]\rangle\ \|\ \mathsf{p}(k_2\backslash K_2)\ \|\ \mathsf{p}(x_1\backslash c_1)\ \|\ \cdots\ \|\ \mathsf{p}(x_l\backslash c_l) \xrightarrow{\to k_2 : E(x_1, \ldots, x_l)}}\ (\mathrm{send}_3)$$
$$\langle K_2,\sigma', s'[E\theta]\rangle\ \|\ \mathsf{p}(k_2\backslash K_2)\ \|\ \mathsf{p}(x_1\backslash c_1)\ \|\ \cdots\ \|\ \mathsf{p}(x_l\backslash c_l)$$

$$\frac{c = F(c_1, \ldots, c_k)}{\langle K,\sigma, s[F(c_1, \ldots, c_k)]\rangle \xrightarrow{\tau} \langle K,\sigma, s[c]\rangle}\ (\mathrm{crypt})\qquad \frac{unbox(c) = i}{\langle K,\sigma, s[\mathsf{unbox}(c)]\rangle \xrightarrow{\tau} \langle K,\sigma, s[i]\rangle}\ (\mathrm{unbox})$$

$$\frac{a \neq K}{\langle K,\sigma, s[\mathsf{newatom}]\rangle \xrightarrow{\tau} \langle K,\sigma, s[a]\rangle\ \|\ \mathsf{g}(a)}\ (\mathrm{newa})\qquad \frac{}{\square \xrightarrow{\nu x} \mathsf{p}(x\backslash a)\ \|\ \mathsf{g}(a)}\ (\mathrm{newn})$$

$$\frac{body(m) = s \qquad s_{task} = s[\bar{c}/params(m)]}{\langle K,\sigma, \mathsf{spawn}\ m(\bar{c}); s\rangle \xrightarrow{\tau} \langle K,\sigma, s\rangle\ \|\ \langle K,\sigma_{init}, s_{task}\rangle}\ (\mathrm{spawn})$$

$$\frac{body(C.run) = s_{init} \qquad K \neq k \in \mathcal{A} \qquad \sigma'(k_{\mathrm{pub}}) = k^+ \qquad \sigma'(k_{\mathrm{priv}}) = k^-}{\langle K,\sigma, s[\mathsf{new}\ C]\rangle \xrightarrow{\tau} \langle K,\sigma, s[k^+]\rangle\ \|\ k^+[C,\sigma']\ \|\ \langle k^+,\sigma'', s_{init}\rangle\ \|\ \mathsf{g}(k)}\ (\mathrm{newc})$$

$$\frac{\triangle \in \{=, \neq\} \qquad E(E_1, \ldots, E_l)\ \triangle\ E'(E_1, \ldots, E_l)}{\mathsf{p}(x_1\backslash E_1)\ \|\ \cdots\ \|\ \mathsf{p}(x_l\backslash E_l) \xrightarrow{E(x_1, \ldots, x_l)\triangle E'(x_1, \ldots, x_l)} \mathsf{p}(x_1\backslash E_1)\ \|\ \cdots\ \|\ \mathsf{p}(x_l\backslash E_l)}\ (\mathrm{eq})$$

$$\frac{P \xrightarrow{\alpha} P' \qquad \mathsf{NV}(P'') \cap \mathsf{NV}(P') = \emptyset}{P\ \|\ P'' \xrightarrow{\alpha} P'\ \|\ P''}\ (\mathrm{frame})$$

Fig. 4. Operational semantics of the target language

describe the generation of new atoms (in $\mathcal{A}$) by the program or by the adversary. In both cases, the newly generated atom is recorded in the configuration. The rule (spawn) describes the spawning of new tasks. The new task belongs to the same object K as the task from where it was spawned. The rule (newc) describes the creation of a new object. As we see, the main method of the newly created object is immediately started.

The rule (eq) allows the adversary to compare messages it has received. These comparisons are the only means for the information to flow from the messages the adversary has received to the state of the adversary. In terms of applied pi calculus, if two states are such that all comparisons the adversary can perform give the same result, then these two states are *statically equivalent* [2, Sec. 4.2].

Finally, we again have the (frame)-rule that allows a transition to happen in a larger context. Similarly to the source language, the context may not interfere with the transition.

We denote the set of all labels occurring in Fig. 4 by Act_{imp}.

5   Translation

For our proposed translation, we need some standard cryptographic operations in our implementation language — symmetric encryption, public-key encryption and signatures. Hence we require the signature Σ to contain the binary operations senc, sdec, penc, pdec, sig and vfy. These are related to each other and to the operations $\cdot^+$ and $\cdot^-$ by the following cancellation rules:

$$\mathsf{pdec}(x^-, \mathsf{penc}(x^+, m)) = m$$
$$\mathsf{sdec}(x, \mathsf{senc}(x, m)) = m$$
$$\mathsf{vfy}(x^+, \mathsf{sig}(x^-, m)) = m,$$

these equalities hold for all messages x and m. Additionally, we need the pairing operation $(\cdot, \cdot)$ and the projections π_1, π_2 with the cancellation rules $\pi_i((x_1, x_2)) = x_i$. Longer tuples can be modeled as the results of repeated applications of pairing. We again stress that we are working in the symbolic (Dolev-Yao, perfect) model of cryptography.

It is possible to check whether a message m is a pair: in this case, m is equal to $(\pi_1(m), \pi_2(m))$. We need similar checks also for encryption and signatures. Hence we require Σ to contain unary operations is_penc?, is_senc? and is_sig?. These are related to the previous operations by cancellation rules $\mathsf{is}_X?(X(\ldots)) = \mathsf{true}$, where $\mathsf{true} \in \Sigma$ is a nullary operation.

We need more complex data types with associated operations for our translation. These types could be simulated by just using the Msg type, and building up the structure using the pairing operations. It may be hard to ensure the atomicity of operations using just the constructs of the implementation language, though. As mutual exclusion is easy to model in π-calculus, we believe that the addition of these data types does not change the straightforwardness of translation from our implementation language to applied pi-calculus.

We let Set be a type that has sets of messages as possible values. We let Map be a type that has finite maps from messages to messages as possible values. We have the operations $\emptyset$: Set, $\{\cdot\}$: Msg $\to$ Set, $\in$: Msg $\times$ Set $\to$ Bool, $\cup, \cap, \backslash$: Set $\times$ Set $\to$ Set for sets. We also have the operations for finite maps: empty : Map, $\cdot[\cdot \mapsto \cdot], \cdot[\cdot \mapsto \cdot]_w$: Map $\times$ Msg^2 $\to$ Map, $\cdot(\cdot)$: Map $\times$ Msg $\to$ Msg, dom : Map $\to$ Set. Here $\varphi[E \mapsto E']_w$ is the *weak update* operation — the value of $\varphi(E)$ is changed only if it was undefined before. If $\varphi(E)$ is undefined then the application $\varphi(E)$ returns null.

We show how to map each program Pr in the source language to the corresponding program $\{\{Pr\}\}$ in the target language. The translation is largely syntax-directed: to translate a program, one has to translate its classes, classes are translated by translating its methods, a method is translated by translating its body, and control statements in the source language have equivalents in the target language. In the following we present the translation of these parts that are not straightforward.

Object fields. In addition to the fields declared in the source program, each object in the implementation language has an additional field φ of type Map. It is initialized to empty and used to store the return values from methods (analogous to futures).

The representation of object and task names is elaborated more in the next paragraphs. Shortly, however: an object is referred to by its public key k^+. Each task is associated with a separate symmetric key K. A reference to a task is stored as a pair (k^+, K) of the keys of the object owning this task, and of this task itself.

The value of the field φ is a finite map that maps pairs of the form (k^+, K) to messages representing the value returned by the task identified by (k^+, K). If $\varphi((k^+, K))$ is undefined then the current object has not yet learned the identity of the task (k^+, K). If $\varphi((k^+, K)) = $ null then the identity has been learned but the message containing the return value has not been parsed.

Types. The types in source and target language are different. We put $\{\{\text{Int}\}\} = \text{Int}$ and $\{\{C\}\} = \{\{\text{Fut}(T)\}\} = \text{Msg}$.

Method invocation. An asynchronous call to an object must be replaced with an explicit message. For simplicity, we assume that a call $e!m(\bar{e})$ does not occur as a subexpression in some larger expression. The statement $v := e_0!m(e_1, \ldots, e_n)$ is translated as follows:

$$x_0 := e_0; \cdots ; x_n := e_n; K := \text{newatom}; v := (x_0, K); \varphi := \varphi[v \mapsto \text{null}];$$
$$\text{send}(x_0, \text{penc}(x_0, (K, m, x_1, \ldots, x_n))) \quad (1)$$

Here $K, x, x_0, \ldots, x_n$ are temporary variables that are not used elsewhere. After computing the values of the expressions $e_0, \ldots, e_n$, we generate a new atom that we store in K, and intend to use as a symmetric key. This is the key that is going to identify the task that is created as the result of the method invocation.

Note the following interesting aspect — the new task is spawned at the object identified by x_0, but the key identifying it is generated at the calling object. This ensures that the key identifying the new task does not have to be communicated back and the "protocol" for invoking a new method consists of a single message only. In this way the translation from the source to the target language is greatly simplified.

After creating the key K, we define the variable v, set the point in the mapping φ storing the values received from other tasks, and send a message to the object identified by x_0. The message lists the invoked method m, its arguments $x_1, \ldots, x_n$, and the identity of the task K.

Method declaration. Compared to the source language, each method of the implementation language receives one additional argument — the symmetric key associated with the task executing that method. The declaration $T\ m(\overline{T\ x})$ is translated into $\{\{T\}\}\ m(\mathsf{Msg}\ K, \overline{\{\{T\}\}\ x})$.

Returning a value. A value returned by a task may be read by anyone knowing the key associated with that task. The reader must be sure of the identity of the object returning the value. The return of the value of the variable v at the end of a method is translated as

$$\mathsf{while}(\mathsf{true})\ \big\{x := \mathsf{newatom}; \mathsf{send}(\mathsf{null}, (k^+, \mathsf{sig}(k^-, \mathsf{senc}(K, (k^+, v, x)))))\big\} \quad (2)$$

Here k^+ and k^- are the fields of the object owning this task, containing this object's public and private keys. The variable K contains the symmetric key associated with this task. We see that the finished task sends out an unbounded number of messages, all different, containing the return value. These messages are receivable by any object.

Getting a returned value. $\{\{v := e.\mathsf{get}\}\}$ is defined as

$$x := e; \varphi := \varphi[x \mapsto \mathsf{null}]_{\mathrm{w}}; \mathsf{while}(\varphi(x) = \mathsf{null})\{\mathsf{skip}\}; v := \varphi(x)$$

(for simplicity we assume that $e.\mathsf{get}$ does not occur as a subexpression).

The main method of an object. Whenever a new object is created, its main method is executed. In our translation, this method is responsible for receiving the messages and acting on them. This method is the same for all classes, only the list of methods it has to consider is different. The method has a local variable ψ of type Set (initially $\emptyset$) that contains the messages that may contain returned values that this object is as of yet incapable of decrypting. It also has a local variable $\mathcal{K}$ of type Set (initially $\emptyset$) that contains the symmetric keys associated with the tasks of this object.

The main method executes an infinite loop that performs the following operations.

- Receive a message from the network, store it in the variable r.
- Let $mc := \mathsf{pdec}(k^-, r)$. If the second component m of mc is equal to the name of some method of class C, and the first component K is not contained in $\mathcal{K}$, then let $v_1, \ldots, v_n$ be the 3rd, 4th, etc. component of mc. Add K to $\mathcal{K}$ and execute $\mathsf{spawn}\ m(K, v_1, \ldots, v_n)$.
- Otherwise we handle r as a returned value. Let $s := \pi_1(r)$ and $vm := \mathsf{vfy}(s, \pi_2(r))$. If the pair (s, vm) is not yet an element of ψ, then add it there.
- For each element (s, vm) of ψ and each (k^+, K) in the domain of φ, such that $\varphi((k^+, K)) = \mathsf{null}$ and $s = k^+$: let $dm = \mathsf{sdec}(K, vm)$. If $\pi_1(dm) = k^+$, then set φ to $\varphi[(k^+, K) \mapsto \pi_2(dm)]$ and remove (s, vm) from ψ. (this step also requires *iterators* over Set and Map)

6   Equivalence

The semantics of programs in both source and implementation language are given as labeled transition systems, albeit with different set of labels. An *adversary* is any other LTS running in parallel and *synchronizing* on (a subset of) these labels. As the labels are different, the possible adversaries are also different and we cannot compare the LTS-s $[\![Pr]\!]$ and $[\![\{\!\{Pr\}\!\}]\!]$ directly. Still, we show that for each program Pr in the source language, $[\![Pr]\!]$ can be translated to one equivalent to $[\![\{\!\{Pr\}\!\}]\!]$ by running a suitable LTS $\mathcal{L}$ in parallel with it. *Vice versa*, $[\![\{\!\{Pr\}\!\}]\!]$ can be translated to one equivalent to $[\![Pr]\!]$ with the help of some LTS $\overleftarrow{\mathcal{L}}$.

Thus, the LTS-s $[\![Pr]\!]$ and $[\![\{\!\{Pr\}\!\}]\!]$ satisfy exactly the same security properties. Indeed, if there were an adversary $\mathcal{A}$ demonstrating the violation of the property $\mathcal{P}$ of the translated program $\{\!\{Pr\}\!\}$ (i.e. the parallel composition of $[\![\{\!\{Pr\}\!\}]\!]$ and $\mathcal{A}$ does not have the property $\mathcal{P}$) then the property $\mathcal{P}$ is also violated for the source program Pr and the parallel composition of $\overleftarrow{\mathcal{L}}$ and $\mathcal{A}$ is the adversary demonstrating this. Similarly, any adversary violating a security property for Pr can be transformed to an adversary violating the same property for $\{\!\{Pr\}\!\}$. The satisfaction of exactly the same security properties means that if we have succeeded to prove that Pr satisfies some security property, then the equivalence result of this section allows us to deduce that $\{\!\{Pr\}\!\}$ also satisfies this property.

The formalization of the claims above requires more definitions. Let $\mathcal{L} = (S, A, \rightarrow, s_0)$ be a LTS. A symmetric relation $\mathcal{R}$ on S is a *branching bisimulation* if for all $s, s', t \in S$ and $\alpha \in A$, $s \xrightarrow{\alpha} s'$ and $s\ \mathcal{R}\ t$ implies either $\alpha = \tau$ and $s'\ \mathcal{R}\ t$, or the existence of $t_1, t_2, t' \in S$, such that $s \xrightarrow{\tau}^* t_1 \xrightarrow{\alpha} t_2 \xrightarrow{\tau}^* t'$, $s\ \mathcal{R}\ t_1$, $s'\ \mathcal{R}\ t_2$, and $s'\ \mathcal{R}\ t'$ [30]. Two states of an LTS are *(branching) bisimilar* if they are related by a branching bisimulation. Two LTS-s $\mathcal{L}_1$ and $\mathcal{L}_2$ are bisimilar (denoted $\mathcal{L}_1 \approx \mathcal{L}_2$) if in their disjoint union, their starting states are bisimilar.

Let $\mathcal{L} = (S, A, \rightarrow, s_0)$ and $\mathcal{L}' = (S', A', \rightarrow', s_0')$ be two LTS-s. Let $B \subseteq (A \cup A') \backslash \{\tau\}$. The *parallel composition* of $\mathcal{L}$ and $\mathcal{L}'$ synchronized on B is a LTS $\mathcal{L} \times_B \mathcal{L}' = (S \times S', (A \cup A') \backslash B, \Rightarrow, (s_0, s_0'))$ where a transition $(s, s') \xrightarrow{\alpha} (t, t')$ exists iff one of the following holds:

- $\alpha \in A$, $s \xrightarrow{\alpha} t$ and $s' = t'$;
- $\alpha \in A'$, $s' \xrightarrow{\alpha}{}' t'$ and $s = t$;
- $\alpha = \tau$ and exists $\beta \in B$, such that $s \xrightarrow{\beta} t$ and $s' \xrightarrow{\beta}{}' t'$.

We can now state the correctness result for our translation. Informally, it states that no behavior of a program Pr is lost, and no new behavior introduced during the translation, as long as these behaviors can be described through branching bisimulation. Hence, if we consider Pr to have some desirable properties, then $\{\{Pr\}\}$ has the same properties.

Theorem 1. *For every program Pr in the source language there exist LTS-s $\overrightarrow{\mathcal{L}}$ and $\overleftarrow{\mathcal{L}}$, such that*

$$[Pr] \times_{Act_{src}} \overrightarrow{\mathcal{L}} \approx [\{\{Pr\}\}]$$
$$[\{\{Pr\}\}] \times_{Act_{imp}} \overleftarrow{\mathcal{L}} \approx [Pr] \ .$$

As an immediate corollary we get an equivalence result similar to [3].

Corollary 1. *Let Pr_1 and Pr_2 be two programs in the source language. Then $[Pr_1] \approx [Pr_2]$ iff $[\{\{Pr_1\}\}] \approx [\{\{Pr_2\}\}]$.*

Proof. Let $[Pr_1] \approx [Pr_2]$. Then $[\{\{Pr_1\}\}] \approx [Pr_1] \times_{Act_{src}} \overrightarrow{\mathcal{L}} \approx [Pr_2] \times_{Act_{src}} \overrightarrow{\mathcal{L}} \approx [\{\{Pr_2\}\}]$. The other direction is analogous. □

The rest of this section is devoted to proving Theorem 1.

6.1   The LTS $\overrightarrow{\mathcal{L}}$

The LTS $\overrightarrow{\mathcal{L}}$ must "translate" the actions of a program Pr in the source language to the actions in Act_{imp}. Also, the environment-initiated actions (belonging to Act_{imp}) must be translated back to the actions in Act_{src} that the program Pr understands.

One may want to specify $\overrightarrow{\mathcal{L}}$ in some programming language. The semantics of this language would then give us an LTS. But only the actual LTS matters for the purposes of the proof, hence we specify it without the detour thorough a programming language. At the same time, we may still think of $\overrightarrow{\mathcal{L}}$ as a machine, executing a program, and having memory. All possible contents of the memory would then be mapped to different states of the LTS. In particular, the LTS $\overrightarrow{\mathcal{L}}$ keeps the following records in the memory:

- A table T that matches the object and task names in source language semantics with the keys in target language semantics. Each entry in this table has the fields *msg* (a cryptographic message denoting the identity of an object or a task, similarly to our translation into the implementation language), *name* (a name in **N** for that object/task in the source language), *type* (a boolean showing whether this entry is for an object or a task name), and *local* (a boolean showing whether this object/task is in the runtime configuration of Pr). If the entry is an object then there is also the field sk for the secret key of that object (in the implementation language). Recall that an object is identified by its public key and a task by a pair of its object's public key and its own symmetric key.

- A (finite) map $\mathbf{P}$ from variables to cryptographic messages, having the same role as the $\mathsf{p}(x\backslash E)$ components in the runtime configurations of the implementation language.
- A set $\mathbf{Ret}$ of pairs (o, n) of object and task names. A pair belongs to this set if the object o in the configuration of the source language has received the return value of the task n that does not belong in that configuration.

With these records, the translation between the source program and the environment for programs in the implementation language is straightforward. If Pr performs a transition labeled with $o \rightarrow o'$, then find the keys k and k' corresponding to o and o' from the table T (if they're not there then generate new name[1] k / k' and add new rows to T), let $E = \mathsf{penc}(k', dummy)$, generate new variables x_1, x_2, x_3, add new bindings $x_1 \mapsto k$, $x_2 \mapsto k'$ and $x_3 \mapsto E$ to $\mathbf{P}$, and perform a transition with the label $x_1 \rightarrow x_2 : x_3$. If Pr performs a transition labeled $o \rightarrow n'[o'.m(\bar{c})]$ then $\overrightarrow{\mathcal{L}}$ similarly finds the keys k and k' of o and o'. It will also translate the names of any objects and futures mentioned in $\bar{c}$ to the cryptographic messages denoting them, generating new names in the process as necessary. As next, $\overrightarrow{\mathcal{L}}$ generates a new name K that will be used as the symmetric key of the new task. It adds K and n' into a new row of the table T. Finally, it prepares a message E as in (1), generates new variables x_1, x_2, x_3, binds k, k', E to them in $\mathbf{P}$, and invokes the transition labeled $x_1 \rightarrow x_2 : x_3$. If keys corresponding to new objects have to be created, then the public key is stored in the field msg and the secret key in the field sk of a new row in the table T.

If $[\![Pr]\!]$ performs a transition labeled $o' \leftarrow o$ then $\overrightarrow{\mathcal{L}}$ finds k and k' denoting these objects, finds the secret key $\tilde{k}$ of the object o from the table T, constructs a message $E = (k, \mathsf{sig}(\tilde{k}, \mathsf{senc}(dummy_1, dummy_2)))$, and indicates the message send as before (performing the transition $x_1 \rightarrow x_2 : x_3$ with x_1, x_2, x_3 bound to k, k', E). The translation of the $n[c] \leftarrow o$ action by $[\![Pr]\!]$ consists of finding the messages k and K denoting the object and task from the table T, translating c (if it is an object/task name), constructing a message E similarly to (2), nondeterministically selecting the recipient k' of the message among the non-local objects in T, and transmitting E from k to k'.

If the environment performs an action $\rightarrow k : E(x_1, \ldots, x_l)$ then $\overrightarrow{\mathcal{L}}$ parses the message $\mathbf{P}(E)$ (note that $\overrightarrow{\mathcal{L}}$ has necessary secret keys for that). If it is an invocation of method m (as in (1)) and no task with the same symmetric key K for the object identified by k_2 has been invoked before, then $\overrightarrow{\mathcal{L}}$ performs the action $n = o!m(\bar{c})$ where $\bar{c}$ is obtained by parsing $\mathbf{P}(E)$ and translating with the help of T. If some object/task names are missing in T, then these are generated

---

[1] The generation of new names is an internal action of $\overrightarrow{\mathcal{L}}$.

with actions νn and νo. Also, $\overrightarrow{\mathcal{L}}$ adds a new row with n and K to T. Similar checks and translations are performed if $\mathbf{P}(E)$ is the return value of some task according to (2). In this case, the set $\mathbf{Ret}$ is additionally consulted and updated.

The LTS $\overrightarrow{\mathcal{L}}$ always has the transitions $E \bigtriangleup E'$ enabled. Here $\bigtriangleup$ is either $=$ or $\neq$, depending on whether $\mathbf{P}(E) = \mathbf{P}(E')$ or not. The transition νx is also always enabled. When it is invoked, $\overrightarrow{\mathcal{L}}$ creates a new name and updates $\mathbf{P}$.

Whenever $\overrightarrow{\mathcal{L}}$ "translates" an action in Act_{src} to an action in Act_{imp} or *vice versa*, it first performs the transition with the label in Act_{imp} (non-deterministically guessing some parameters, if necessary), and afterwards the transition with the label in Act_{src}. This keeps the branching behaviors of $[\![Pr]\!] \times_{Act_{\text{src}}} \overrightarrow{\mathcal{L}}$ and $[\![\{\{Pr\}\}]\!]$ the same.

6.2   The LTS $\overleftarrow{\mathcal{L}}$

The LTS $\overleftarrow{\mathcal{L}}$ translates the actions of a program in the implementation language to the actions in Act_{src}. We do not have to consider all programs in the implementation language, but only those of the form $\{\{Pr\}\}$, where Pr is a program in the source language.

Internally, $\overleftarrow{\mathcal{L}}$ keeps the following records.

- The table T^o relates the cryptographic messages with object names in $\mathbf{N}$ (note that creating new names in $\mathbf{N}$ is under the control of $\overleftarrow{\mathcal{L}}$). Each entry in this table has the field *name* for storing the name $o \in \mathbf{N}$. It also has the field *msg* that contains the cryptographic expression (with variables) that evaluates to the public key of that object if these variables are substituted with the messages associated with them by the runtime configuration of $\{\{Pr\}\}$ (through the $\mathsf{p}(x\backslash E)$-parts).
- The table T^{myo} relates the object identities and names for those objects that $\overleftarrow{\mathcal{L}}$ itself has caused to be created. It has the fields *var* and *name* with the latter having the same meaning as in T^o. The field *var* contains the variable whose value is an atomic message, such that var^+ is the public key and var^- the secret key of the object.
- The table T^t relates the cryptographic messages with task names in $\mathbf{N}$. Each entry in this table has the fields *name*, msg^t and msg^o. The two *msg*-fields contain cryptographic expressions that resolve to the symmetric key identifying the task, and public key of the owning object, respectively.
- The table $\mathbf{Ret}$ having the same role as in $\overrightarrow{\mathcal{L}}$.

The transitions of $[\![\{\{Pr\}\}]\!]$ and the environment (which makes transitions labeled with elements of Act_{src}) are translated as follows. If $\{\{Pr\}\}$ performs a transition labeled with $k_1 \rightarrow k_2 : x$ then $\overleftarrow{\mathcal{L}}$ finds the objects o_1 and o_2 corresponding to the keys k_1 and k_2 by comparing k_i with $R.msg$ for all entries R in T^o. The comparison is performed with the help of $[\![\{\{Pr\}\}]\!]$, by attempting the transitions labeled with $k_i \bigtriangleup R.msg$ for $\bigtriangleup \in \{=, \neq\}$. If T^o does not contain k_1 or k_2 then a new entry is added to T^o with a new name from $\mathbf{N}$. If o_2 is not in T^{myo} then this message is between two objects in the runtime configuration of $\{\{Pr\}\}$. It will be translated either as $o_1 \to o_2$ or $o_2 \leftarrow o_1$, depending on the structure of the message pointed to by x.

If o_2 is in T^{myo}, then the message x is from an object in the runtime configuration of $\{\{Pr\}\}$ to an object outside it. If it is a method call then $\overleftarrow{\mathcal{L}}$ can decrypt the message x because it has the secret key corresponding to k_2. It finds the method m to be called, the symmetric key K identifying the task that the object o_2 is supposed to spawn, as well as the arguments $\bar{c}$. The arguments can be decoded with the help of the tables T^o and T^t. The LTS $\overleftarrow{\mathcal{L}}$ will generate a new task name n, add a new entry (n, K, k_2) to the table T^t and perform the transition labeled with $o_1 \to n[o_2.m(\overline{c_{decoded}})]$. Similarly, if x is the return of a value then it can be decrypted because the symmetric key K of the task that returned it can be found in T^t (see below for handling method calls coming from the environment). The task name n is found from the entry containing K and k_1, the returned value c is decoded and the transition $n[c_{decoded}] \leftarrow o_1$ is performed.

If the environment performs a transition labeled with $n = o!m(\bar{c})$ then $\overleftarrow{\mathcal{L}}$ will add a new entry to the table T^t with n, the public key k of the object o (found from T^o) and a new symmetric key K, obtained by performing a transition labeled with νx. It will then encode the arguments $\bar{c}$ with the help of the tables T^o and T^t. If some of the arguments are missing from these tables then new entries are added, obtaining the necessary keys through transitions labeled with νx. The LTS $\overleftarrow{\mathcal{L}}$ will then construct a new message E in the shape of (1) and perform a transition labeled with $\to k : E$.

If the environment performs a transition labeled with $o \leftarrow n[c]$ with o being found in T^o and n in T^t, and the pair (n, o) not belonging to **Ret** (if some of these conditions do not hold then $\overleftarrow{\mathcal{L}}$ will have no such transition for the environment to synchronize upon) then $\overleftarrow{\mathcal{L}}$ finds from T^t the symmetric key k^+ of the object having executed the task n. The object was running in the environment, thus its secret key can be found from T^{myo}. The LTS $\overleftarrow{\mathcal{L}}$ will now construct a message E according to (2) and perform a transition labeled with $\to k_o : E$, where k_o is the public key of o found from T^o.

If the environment performs a transition labeled with νo then $\overleftarrow{\mathcal{L}}$ will obtain a new key k by performing a transition labeled with νx, add (k, o) to the table T^{myo} and (o, k^+) to the table T^o. If the environment performs a transition labeled with νn then $\overleftarrow{\mathcal{L}}$ will obtain new keys K and k by performing two transitions labeled with νx. It will generate a new name $o \in \mathbf{N}$, add the entry (k, o) to T^{myo}, the entry (o, k^+) to T^o and (n, K, k^+) to T^t. This is a valid translation for names of tasks controlled *and initiated* by the environment because a program Pr has no means to make sure whether two of such tasks are executed by the same object or by different objects.

Similarly to $\overrightarrow{\mathcal{L}}$, whenever $\overleftarrow{\mathcal{L}}$ "translates" an action in Act_{imp} to an action in Act_{src} or *vice versa*, it first performs the transition with the label in Act_{src} and afterwards the transition with the label in Act_{imp}.

6.3   Bisimulations

The reachable states of the LTS $[\![Pr]\!] \times_{Act_{src}} \overrightarrow{\mathcal{L}}$ satisfy invariants stating that the runtime configuration C of $[\![Pr]\!]$ and the data $(T, \mathbf{P}, \mathbf{Ret})$ kept by $\overrightarrow{\mathcal{L}}$ are consistent. Namely, T contains an entry about the object o or task n iff $\mathsf{p}(o) \in C$ or $\mathsf{p}(n) \in C$. The values of the fields *local* and *type* match with the type and locality of the elements in C. A pair (o, n) is in $\mathbf{Ret}$ iff $o.\varphi(n)$ is defined. The data kept by $\overrightarrow{\mathcal{L}}$ provides an easy translation between the states S of $[\![Pr]\!] \times_{Act_{src}} \overrightarrow{\mathcal{L}}$ and the states C' of $[\![\{\{Pr\}\}]\!]$, giving us a bisimulation between these LTSs. Roughly, the states $S = (C, T, \mathbf{P}, \mathbf{Ret})$ and C' are related iff there exists a permutation θ of $\mathcal{A}$, such that

- C and C' have the same objects with the same names (public keys), where the translation between object names and public keys is given by T and θ. For an object name o, if T contains an entry R with $R.name = o$, then the object $o[\ldots] \in C$ corresponds to the object $(T.msg)\theta[\ldots] \in C'$. Objects $o[\ldots] \in C$ with names o not occurring in T correspond to objects $k^+[\ldots] \in C'$ with $k^+(\theta^{-1})$ not occurring in T in arbitrary one-to-one manner. Two corresponding objects must have the same class and the same values for their fields. For fields of type "object" or "task", the translation is again given through T and θ. The component φ of an object in C must match with the union of the field φ of the corresponding object in C', and the local variable ψ in this object's task executing the main method.
- C and C' have the same tasks (except for the tasks executing the main methods of objects in C'). Again, the translation between task names and symmetric keys is given by T and θ with tasks not present in T mapped to each other. A task's symmetric key is stored in its first input parameter. The local variables of the corresponding tasks have the same values, and the execution is at the same program point.
- The mapping $\mathbf{P}$ matches the elements $\mathsf{p}(x\backslash E)$ in C': for some $x \in \mathcal{X}$, $\mathbf{P}(x)$ is defined iff $p(x\backslash E) \in C'$ for some E. Moreover, $\mathbf{P}(x)\theta = E$.

The use of the permutation θ is justified by the fact that actual atomic messages in $\mathcal{A}$ are inaccessible to environments synchronizing over Act_{imp}. This avoids the problem that keys $k \in \mathcal{A}$ identifying objects are created at different times in $[\![\{\{Pr\}\}]\!]$ and $[\![Pr]\!] \times_{Act_{src}} \overrightarrow{\mathcal{L}}$ (time of creation vs. time of becoming public). These identifiers are accessed through variables which are created at the same time in both LTSs (time of becoming public).

The bisimulation between $[\![\{\{Pr\}\}]\!] \times_{Act_{imp}} \overleftarrow{\mathcal{L}}$ and $[\![Pr]\!]$ is similar. Again, the reachable states of $[\![\{\{Pr\}\}]\!] \times_{Act_{imp}} \overleftarrow{\mathcal{L}}$ satisfy consistency invariants: if C' is the runtime configuration of $[\![\{\{Pr\}\}]\!]$ and $(T^o, T^{myo}, T^t, \mathbf{Ret})$ is the internal state of $\overleftarrow{\mathcal{L}}$, then an entry R in T^o means that an object with the public key $R.msg$ is a component of C', unless $R.msg$ also occurs in T^{myo}. The states $S' = (C', T^o, T^{myo}, T^t, \mathbf{Ret})$ and C are related, if

- C' and C have the same objects, where the translation between object names and public keys is given by T^o. These objects must be equivalent — have the same class and values of fields, including the component/field φ and the local variable ψ of the main method of the object. The objects in C' whose public keys are not present in T^o are mapped to the objects o in C where $\mathsf{p}(o)$ is not part of the configuration C.

- C and S' know the same objects in the environment. For each row R in T^{myo} there is a component $\mathsf{p}(R.name)$ in C without the object $R.name[\ldots]$ itself being a component of C. Similarly, if there exists an object name o, such that $\mathsf{p}(o)$ is part of C, but $o[\ldots]$ is not, then there is a row R of T^{myo}, such that $R.name = o$.

- C' and C have the same tasks (except for the tasks executing the main methods of objects in C'), where the translation between task names and symmetric keys is given through T^t. Tasks in C with names not occurring in T^t are matched with tasks in C' with keys not occurring in T^t. If there is an entry (n, K, k^+) in T^t, but there is no task K of the object k^+ running in C', then there is also no task $n\langle\ldots\rangle$ in C, but $\mathsf{p}(n)$ is a component of C.

7   Conclusions

We have shown how to translate a distributed object-oriented language arising in the programming language and formal verification community to (a dialect of) applied pi calculus, such that the security properties of programs are preserved. Compared to other similar results, our source language does not so explicitly include communication between processes in different locations. Rather, the communication happens when needed to execute the language constructs. In this sense, the gap our translation has to cross is larger. On the other hand, this may also simplify the translation because it somewhat restricts the possible communication patterns. Still, the "channels" (object references and futures) can be freely communicated and this requires some non-obvious tricks to securely translate.

Besides the security, other aspects of implementing ABS are also worthy of studying. In parallel to our work, the *routing* of messages (which is made highly non-trivial by the fact that futures are first-class values and a finishing task does not know where its result is needed), as well as the mobility of objects is being studied by Dam and Palmskog [14].

References

1. Abadi, M.: Protection in Programming-Language Translations. In: Larsen, K.G., Skyum, S., Winskel, G. (eds.) ICALP 1998. LNCS, vol. 1443, pp. 868–883. Springer, Heidelberg (1998)
2. Abadi, M., Fournet, C.: Mobile values, new names, and secure communication. In: POPL, pp. 104–115 (2001)
3. Abadi, M., Fournet, C., Gonthier, G.: Secure Implementation of Channel Abstractions. In: LICS, pp. 105–116. IEEE Computer Society (1998)

4. Abadi, M., Fournet, C., Gonthier, G.: Secure Communications Processing for Distributed Languages. In: IEEE Symposium on Security and Privacy, pp. 74–88 (1999)
5. Abadi, M., Fournet, C., Gonthier, G.: Authentication Primitives and Their Compilation. In: POPL, pp. 302–315 (2000)
6. Ábrahám, E., Grabe, I., Grüner, A., Steffen, M.: Behavioral interface description of an object-oriented language with futures and promises. J. Log. Algebr. Program. 78(7), 491–518 (2009)
7. Adão, P., Fournet, C.: Cryptographically Sound Implementations for Communicating Processes. In: Bugliesi, M., Preneel, B., Sassone, V., Wegener, I. (eds.) ICALP 2006. Part II. LNCS, vol. 4052, pp. 83–94. Springer, Heidelberg (2006)
8. Backes, M., Cortesi, A., Focardi, R., Maffei, M.: A calculus of challenges and responses. In: Ning, P., Atluri, V., Gligor, V.D., Mantel, H. (eds.) FMSE, pp. 51–60. ACM (2007)
9. Bugliesi, M., Focardi, R.: Language based secure communication. In: CSF, pp. 3–16. IEEE Computer Society (2008)
10. Bugliesi, M., Giunti, M.: Secure implementations of typed channel abstractions. In: Hofmann, M., Felleisen, M. (eds.) POPL, pp. 251–262. ACM (2007)
11. Clarke, D., Diakov, N., Hähnle, R., Johnsen, E.B., Puebla, G., Weitzel, B., Wong, P.Y.H.: Hats - a formal software product line engineering methodology. In: Botterweck, G., Jarzabek, S., Kishi, T., Lee, J., Livengood, S. (eds.) SPLC Workshops, pp. 121–128. Lancaster University (2010)
12. Clarke, D., Diakov, N., Hähnle, R., Johnsen, E.B., Schaefer, I., Schäfer, J., Schlatte, R., Wong, P.Y.H.: Modeling Spatial and Temporal Variability with the HATS Abstract Behavioral Modeling Language. In: Bernardo, M., Issarny, V. (eds.) SFM 2011. LNCS, vol. 6659, pp. 417–457. Springer, Heidelberg (2011)
13. Comon-Lundh, H., Cortier, V.: Computational soundness of observational equivalence. In: Ning, P., Syverson, P.F., Jha, S. (eds.) ACM Conference on Computer and Communications Security, pp. 109–118. ACM (2008)
14. Dam, M., Palmskog, K.: A Foundation for Network-Adaptive Execution of Distributed Objects (work in progress, 2012)
15. Dolev, D., Yao, A.C.-C.: On the Security of Public Key Protocols. IEEE Transactions on Information Theory 29(2), 198–207 (1983)
16. Fournet, C., Gonthier, G.: The reflexive chemical abstract machine and the join-calculus. In: POPL, pp. 372–385 (1996)
17. Fournet, C., Rezk, T.: Cryptographically Sound Implementations for Typed Information-Flow Security. In: Proceedings of the 35th ACM SIGPLAN-SIGACT Symposium on Principles of Programming Languages, POPL 2008. ACM Press, San Francisco (2008)
18. Goldwasser, S., Micali, S.: Probabilistic Encryption. Journal of Computer and System Sciences 28(2), 270–299 (1984)
19. Hähnle, R.: HATS: Highly Adaptable and Trustworthy Software Using Formal Methods. In: Margaria, T., Steffen, B. (eds.) ISoLA 2010, Part II. LNCS, vol. 6416, pp. 3–8. Springer, Heidelberg (2010)
20. Hähnle, R., Johnsen, E.B., Østvold, B.M., Schäfer, J., Steffen, M., Torjusen, A.B.: Report on the Core ABS Language and Methodology: Part A. Highly Adaptable and Trustworthy Software using Formal Models (HATS), Deliverable D1.1A (April 2010)
21. Helvensteijn, M., Muschevici, R., Wong, P.Y.H.: Delta modeling in practice: a Fredhopper case study. In: Eisenecker, U.W., Apel, S., Gnesi, S. (eds.) VaMoS, pp. 139–148. ACM (2012)

22. Johnsen, E.B., et al.: ABS: A Core Language for Abstract Behavioral Specification. In: Aichernig, B.K., de Boer, F.S., Bonsangue, M.M. (eds.) FMCO 2010. LNCS, vol. 6957, pp. 142–164. Springer, Heidelberg (2011)
23. Johnsen, E.B., Owe, O., Yu, I.C.: Creol: A type-safe object-oriented model for distributed concurrent systems. Theoretical Computer Science 365(1-2), 23–66 (2006)
24. Jones, C.B.: A pi-Calculus Semantics for an Object-Based Design Notation. In: Best, E. (ed.) CONCUR 1993. LNCS, vol. 715, pp. 158–172. Springer, Heidelberg (1993)
25. Milner, R.: Communicating and mobile systems: the π-calculus. Cambridge University Press (1999)
26. Mödersheim, S., Viganò, L.: Secure Pseudonymous Channels. In: Backes, M., Ning, P. (eds.) ESORICS 2009. LNCS, vol. 5789, pp. 337–354. Springer, Heidelberg (2009)
27. Philippsen, M.: A survey of concurrent object-oriented languages. Concurrency: Practice and Experience 12(10), 917–980 (2000)
28. Schaefer, I., Hähnle, R.: Formal methods in software product line engineering. IEEE Computer 44(2), 82–85 (2011)
29. Schneider, J.-G., Lumpe, M.: Synchronizing Concurrent Objects in the π-Calculus. In: Ducournau, R., Garlatti, S. (eds.) Proceedings of Languages et Modèles à Objets, Hermes, Roscoff, pp. 61–76 (1997)
30. van Glabbeek, R.J., Weijland, W.P.: Branching Time and Abstraction in Bisimulation Semantics. Journal of the ACM 43(3), 555–600 (1996)
31. Vaughan, J.A., Zdancewic, S.: A cryptographic decentralized label model. In: IEEE Symposium on Security and Privacy, pp. 192–206. IEEE Computer Society (2007)

Establishing Trust between Nodes in Mobile Ad-Hoc Networks[*]

Nicolai Kuntze[1], Carsten Rudolph[1], and Janne Paatero[2]

[1] Fraunhofer SIT
{nicolai.kuntze,carsten.rudolph}@sit.fraunhofer.de
[2] RUAG
Janne.Paatero@ruag.com

Abstract. Civil protection organizations like firefighters or police rely on mobile personnel capable of solving tasks in exceptional scenarios. Wireless mobile and ad-hoc communication equipment can be used to support operations in areas of collapsed or unavailable communication infrastructures. Mobile ad-hoc networks rely on routing protocols where each individual device becomes a node of the network. Existing routing protocols concentrate on establishing an efficient distribution of routing information and on routing of messages. However, the particular properties of mobile ad-hoc networks enable various new attacks, in particular targeting routing. Conventional security mechanisms fail to cope with the arising security challenges. Identification of each device and trust relationships between devices become an important function of the complete network. This paper proposes to apply well-known security mechanisms and concepts from the domain of trusted computing in order to establish trust between devices. Attestation of devices is integrated into the mobile ad-hoc network routing protocol and building on this, transmission of routing- and payload data can be restricted to identified devices in trustworthy states. Thus, malicious devices can be automatically recognized by all devices and excluded from participation in the network. Especially the dissemination of misleading routing information, which affects the availability of the whole network, is effectively prevented. A prototypical implementation and first tests in a mobile ad-hoc network test-bed, consisting of nodes equipped with a Trusted Platform Module, demonstrate the feasibility of the approach. The challenges and room for improvement in terms of timing and efficiency are also discussed.

1 Introduction

None of the currently available mobile ad-hoc network (MANET) protocols support the establishment of trust between network devices. Nevertheless, as each device in a MANET also serves as a network node responsible for routing, mutual trust between devices is even more relevant than in other static networks. Obviously, existing security protocols could be used to establish trust between

---

[*] This work was partially supported by the SecFutur EU FP7 project.

C.J. Mitchell and A. Tomlinson (Eds.): INTRUST 2012, LNCS 7711, pp. 48–62, 2012.
© Springer-Verlag Berlin Heidelberg 2012

nodes. However, attacks on MANETs can be based on the link layer and particularly on routing information. Routing information is exchanged directly during the joining process of a node. Furthermore, nodes can change their location and may frequently leave or re-join. Therefore, the trust between devices also needs to follow this dynamic characteristic of the MANET.

Many typical security threats, including malware such as viruses, root-kits, Trojans or targeted software attacks, are also applicable to MANET nodes. Through manipulated or malicious nodes so-called wormholes, black-holes, flooding and many other attacks become possible and are known to seriously disrupt network services [7]. Further, mobile devices, as used by civil protection organisations, must operate in a potentially malicious environment. Such an environment introduces additional attack vectors. Especially MANETs are highly vulnerable to the mentioned threats, since they do not have any central nodes where protection can be concentrated. They need to be flexible and operate without strongly protected infrastructural systems. Immediate exclusion is crucial in a network where all participants act as routers. In case of *Push-to-talk* (PTT) scenarios, malicious systems may otherwise gain a tremendous influence on the communication between the actors in the field.

Security in MANETs is an active area of research. Most work in this area covers the integrity of routing tables under the assumption that communication devices are trustworthy or only a limited number of devices are malicious [2,4]. These approaches are for example based on simulation models [12] or use biologically inspired concepts [11]. MANET devices use wireless, standardised communication technology. Thus, the implicit assumption of trustworthiness no longer reflects the real security threat. Furthermore, devices might be compromised before the actual critical mission starts.

Within this paper, concepts from the domain of Trusted Computing (TC) [13] are used to provide a solution for the establishment of trust between nodes of mobile ad-hoc networks. The approach supports secure routing- and payload transmission between neighbours, as well as authentication and attestation of neighbours. Here, neighbours are nodes in the MANET that are in range of a single transmission device. In the proposed *MANET of trustworthy members* (TrustMANET), each member can independently exclude suspicious neighbours from participation. Such a mechanism provides reliable link information to higher layer services (e.g. voice call routing). The approach aims at *Push-to-talk* PTT voice communication and MANET but can also be applied in related scenarios. Some concepts for using TC in the context of MANETs have been proposed before but with different goals. One approach presented by Xu at al. [19] uses a protocol from Goldman et al. [5] to bind a session key to a TPM-based attestation. The key is a symmetric key shared by all nodes in the network. This approach is useful to establish secure groups more on the application level. It is not suitable for scenarios with frequents dynamic changes in mobile ad-hoc networks. In contrast to these existing protocols, the TrustMANET protocol protects single hops to neighbors in the network. Thus, malicious nodes can be directly excluded before routing information is exchanged and also frequent re-attestation is supported. Another approach by Krishna et al. [9] proposes a very limited trusted computing base, that basically can do symmetric verification. The term Trusted Computing Base is misleading as the proposed module is rather a crypto co-processor. The achieved security, based on public keys, is rather low. No secure node identification or node attestation is involved.

The following section presents a motivating scenario and introduces basic terms from the domain of TC as well as from the B.A.T.M.A.N. routing protocol [6]. A security analysis of the scenario and derived requirements are provided in Section 3. Section 4 includes the most important aspects of the communication and system architecture. Elements of a communication device are described as well as the definition of a new protocol. System tables and message flows are specified from a general perspective. Finally, an outlook summarises current and future research activities.

2   Background

2.1   Push-to-Talk

Some MANET applications use single routes through the network. However, in many practical MANET scenarios the goal is to use as many routes as possible. These applications are particularly vulnerable to attacks on MANET routing. *Push-to-talk* (PTT) describes a communication principle that is suitable for fast and easy communication within closed groups. Members of such a group own a broadcast voice channel, allowing them to talk and send information to the whole group by triggering a single control button. In practice, PTT is applied in areas such as construction workers, fire fighters, police forces, transport services for goods or passengers and many other use cases. PTT is just one example of an application with strong requirements with respect to the underlying communication channels. As far as possible, operations in the field should be independent from central infrastructures, central services and the availability of any single member. The availability within the network can be increased by dedicated relay equipment. It enables organizations to operate a MANET in a broader area usually restricted by the limits of user devices. Group members may drop relay devices at proper locations and collect them at the end of the operation. Such devices do not have to be different from user devices, however it will be more practicable to introduce relay devices with distinguished capabilities, but with restricted interaction and less (hardware) interfaces for users.

An advanced version of such a MANET should allow users to configure the required *Quality of Service* (QoS). We extend this concept by introducing trust measures as an additional metric for an enhanced view on quality. In practice, critical information has to be transmitted on routes that can be different to those used for usual operation. Thus, also low quality (or "insecure") channels can be used for information with low security requirements or for emergency communication when high-quality channels are not available.

2.2   Trusted Computing

Trusted Computing (TC) as it is described by the TC Group offers a variety of security concepts that are intended to establish a higher level of security amongst *Information and Communication Technology* (ICT) systems. Especially the *Trusted Platform Module* (TPM) [18] can provide a powerful and hard to penetrate root of trust. Such a hardware security module can serve as the basis for identifying nodes in a MANET. Furthermore, it can also be used as the root of trust for measuring the status of the individual nodes in terms of software installed and running and in terms of configurations. The architecture of the TPM is similar to what is known from smart-card technologies. the TPM provides proper hardware random number generation, cryptographic operations, non-volatile storage for root keys, volatile registers for keys loaded for use and hash chains representing the history of measurement values since the last reset of the TPM (typically since the last reboot), and finally I/O interfaces. Implemented as an on-board hardware chip, it serves as a reliable source of trust. However, just fitting a TPM on the MANET node's mainboard will not satisfy any security requirements. A *Trusted Computing System* (TCS) is a device that is equipped with such a TPM and additionally provides booting routines for trustworthy system start, a trustworthy operating system and trustworthy applications. Starting from the hardware-based TPM, a TCS is able to track all subsequently activated software components in a reliable way and provide reports on these measurements. As these reports are protected by the TPM, they cannot be compromised by software means. In practice, a proper *trust model* for these measurement processes must be defined. Such a trust model d- on requirements of certain use cases and it determines which com-   .s (e.g. binaries of boot routines) are subject to measurement and wh·   .not. A TCS preserves hash values of measured components in the   . *Measurement Log* (SML). TPMs are capable to report and sign su·¹   .em state. This process is called (*attestation*) and with the help of °-   .ate protocols, the attested state can be provided to and verified bv   . systems using the process of (*remote attestation*). So-called *Attest*   .entity Keys* (AIK) can provide pseudonyms or uniquely identify node,   .ing the attestation process, if the relation of the AIK to a TPM's endorsement key is known. The approach presented here concentrates on protecting the routing. A survey on other possible uses of trusted computing for MANETS can be found in [10].

2.3   B.A.T.M.A.N

The described push-to-talk application scenarios require a light-weight ad-hoc routing protocol, capable of coping with very dynamic mesh-networks without central access points in the range of participating nodes. The *Better Approach To Mobile Ad-hoc Networking* (BATMAN) [14] has turned out to be a very promising candidate for this purpose. BATMAN acquires routing information from neighbouring nodes in a *Distance-Vector Routing* like manner where no single node needs to know the topology of the whole network. Instead, a proactive flooding mechanism is applied to acquire the neighbouring node that has the best connection (metric in terms of quality) to a destination node. Especially, the amount of received routing packages within a certain period of time determines a concrete value of the metric. Effects of changes in the network topology remain local. In exchange, packets can't be routed on pre-set paths. Connectivity to other networks is provided by designated bridging nodes. Such nodes do not differ from others, except that they announce themselves as a gateway in each direction. Incorporated in the Data Link Layer, BATMAN establishes connections and carries payload from higher layer protocols such as IP or ARP.

3   Security Considerations

We aim for achieving a security enhanced MANET protocol according to the following main objectives. They refer to threats that are relevant in practice. A concept for a secure BATMAN is described in subsequent chapters.

Protection of Communication Channels

In MANETs, communication between wireless devices is realized via an open broadcast medium. Compatible devices, in the range of a sending device, are capable to receive all contents of the transmission. Furthermore, they are capable of sending similar or equal contents on the medium. So far, security was not in the focus of the design of these networks. The proposed concept implements mechanisms for the protection of communication channels. It achieves confidentiality of all transmitted data on a hop-by-hop (direct link) basis and it protects from eavesdropping. Authentication and integrity assessment of a remote device precedes any data transmission. Further mechanisms, such as wearable biosensors [17] providing advanced authentication mechanisms between devices, can seamlessly be integrated in the proposed architecture. Such biosensors provide advanced authentication mechanisms between device and user in order to prevent misuse of devices. However, they are not in focus of this paper. Protected communication channels are established in the field. All devices within transmission range exchange shared secrets for the protection of transmissions. The key-exchange mechanism also uses the TPM whereby a hardware protection against man-in-the-middle like threats is implemented.

3.1   Protection of Privacy

The provided solution can be employed in a way that it protects information on the identity of a device against peers. Unintended traceability, recognition and assignment of single device, and thereby its user, is precluded on the link-layer. Pseudonymous TPM keys, the secured key exchange and transmission mechanisms support the protection of privacy. Solutions on higher and lower communication layers, as well as revealing device characteristics can of course add additional identity information, but if a device can already be uniquely identified on the link layer, pseudonymity in a MANET cannot be established on higher levels. [8].

3.2 Protection of Routing Tables

Proper operation of MANETs mainly relies on routing tables. They have to be protected from manipulation in order to counter a variety of threats. Unsecured MANETs suffer from outsider and insider attacks, aiming to inject wrong routing information into the routing tables. In both cases, the dissemination of manipulated routing information must be prevented. For our solution it is assumed that devices with a correct software state do not manipulate routing information. Thus, attacks either come from outsider devices or from software manipulation on known devices. The TPM, integrated in each device, and its integrity measurement mechanisms allow devices to recognize manipulations on neighbour devices. Routing messages of manipulated devices are dropped and not forwarded in the network.

3.3 Protection of Cryptographic Keys

Capturing of devices by an adversary is a serious concern for mobile equipment. Especially, pre-shared keys need to be protected even if devices are stolen. The provided solution does not require any pre-shared and MANET-wide symmetric keys which are expected to increase the vulnerability of the whole network. Instead it relies on asymmetric keys stored on the TPM. Identity keys and storage keys cannot be compromised by software means. Physical manipulations to TPMs are possible but difficult, expensive and time consuming. All other cryptographic keys utilized in the communication between devices are freshly created, bound to a well known system state and of short temporal validity.

4 Architecture

A MANET consists of directly connected mobile nodes. In order to meet the requirements in Section 3 we envision an operational model that enforces the trustworthiness of the devices within the network. In such an infrastructure, each device is capable of recognising untrustworthy devices and of rejecting subsequent communication attempts. Manipulated devices become isolated and can be redirected to a "quarantine zone" where they have to undergo remediation procedures.

This section presents concepts for trustworthy MANETs on the basis of off-the-shelf technologies. It is assumed that all devices pass through a set-up process (e.g. briefing or roll-out). A so called "take ownership" procedure embodies certain credentials in the device. Based on this set-up process, a group of nodes are able to form a trustworthy MANET in the field. A high level introduction of the operational model is given below and Section 4.2 presents a modified BATMAN protocol. The proposed architecture and protocols are of general nature. However, the BATMAN integrated implementation serves as a good baseline for detailed analysis. The impact on the routing messages is shown in Section 4.3 and subsequent modifications to the routing tables are presented in Section 4.4. Section 4.5 suggests a mechanism for frequently renewing of the random values in broadcast messages initiating the handshake between devices.

4.1 High Level Architecture

Trust in the communication device requires knowledge of the correct function of a device's hardware and software components. Attacks on hardware components can be encountered by specific design approaches not in the focus of this paper. Software attacks are more complex to mitigate in comparison. Devices become TC Systems (see Section 2.2) with the capability of measuring and attesting their state to remote devices (neighbours). Figure 1 depicts the high level system design from the perspective of the routing protocol. An operating system capable of integrity measurement (e.g. [15]) is expected to be in place.

The design of the Linux based operating systems is modular. User Space software is decoupled from Kernel Space software and hardware devices. The described routing functionality is mainly based on a Wireless-Device and the TPM. Apart from elementary kernel routines, additional modules extend the kernel functionality and manage attached devices such as the TPM at the *Low Pin Count* (LPC)-Bus or the wireless devices at the *Peripheral Component Interconnect* (PCI)-Bus. The kernel provides various interfaces (eth0/wlan0, file system, NetLink, /dev/tpm) to applications in the User Space. Inter Process Communication (IPC) allows exchange of data between User Space applications.

Basic MANET functionality (routing, forwarding and neighbour discovery) of the BATMAN kernel module is reused in the `TrustMANET-Module`. The architecture integrates the advanced version of BATMAN. All network interfaces for applications (`eth0/wlan0`) and the interface to the Wireless-Device remain unchanged. Related software applications can be operated without modification. Security features are incorporated in a `TrustMANET-Management` and a `TrustMANET-Daemon`. These components are decoupled from the kernel module in order to separate functionality that is not specific to lower layers.

The `TrustMANET-Module` processes all valid incoming link-layer traffic and it dispatches encrypted and security related content to the dæmon where subsequent cryptographic operations are performed. The dæmon is responsible for processing handshake protocol messages between neighbours, and subsequent encryption of network traffic. It accesses functionality of the TPM and it computes all related validation and verification tasks. If content is addressed to the local system, it is decrypted and given back to the module for further possessing as provided by BATMAN Other content is re-encrypted according to the addressed system.

4.2 Protocol Design

The set-up procedure for devices is expected to be conducted in a fully controlled and secured environment. Each device obtains own asymmetric AIK pairs (public and private key) and one certified public key for each operative device. These keys are applied in the operative environment during the TrustMANET handshake as described in the following protocol message sequence (see Table 1). Another option is to use certified AIKs and only establish on the nodes the certificate of the certification authority. This approach scales better, but revocation is more difficult (e.g. AIKs of stolen devices need to be blacklisted on each node).

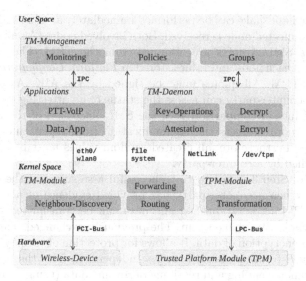

Fig. 1. TrustMANET (TM) Device-Architecture

The TrustMANET protocol establishes protected links between pairs of trustworthy neighbours. Such TrustMANET-Links allow senders to securely transmit typical BATMAN data and routing information whereby common outsider attacks on routing tables can be prevented. Nodes achieve a TrustMANET-Link to a neighbour with completion of a cryptographic handshake. The handshake defines three processing steps and three types of messages. With completion of the protocol steps, a pair of neighbouring nodes have accomplished: (i) authentication of the counter-party, (ii) verification of the counter-party integrity, and (iii) exchange of shared secrets. If anonymity is required, Direct Anonymous Attestation [1]) can be used. None of the transmitted messages are relayed in the network until the handshake is completed. Table 1 depicts the required message flow.

Nodes (A and B in step 1) that are not yet connected, frequently and asynchronously broadcast *TrustMANET Calls* (TMC). Such calls contain a fresh random number (S_{pub}^A) and an encrypted routing message, called *Originator Message* (OGM). The routing message remains inaccessible until completion of the handshake. Already connected nodes do not have to process a handshake again. They can just extract the routing updates (OGM) for further processing. Not yet connected nodes simultaneously exchange random numbers within TMC messages. The pair of random numbers ($S_{pub}^A = g^x, S_{pub}^B = g^y$) is applied to create a shared secret ($S^{AB} = g^{xy}$) between A and B as it is described by the *Diffie-Hellman* (DH) key exchange algorithm [3]. It is to be noted that the random numbers have to be chosen according to the DH protocol. In order to limit potential attacks on the DH algorithm or the freshness of messages, we introduce a mechanism that frequently renews the random numbers (see Section 4.5). However, renewing of the random number (S_{pub}^A) does not require to re-establish shared secrets between already connected devices.

Step 2 of the handshake can be performed immediately after a random number S_{pub} of an unconnected node is received. Both involved nodes (A and B) transmit a quote and a SML. Quotes are obtained from the TPM. They include the random value of each node and values stored in *Platform Configuration Registers* (PCR) of the TPM. All quotes must be signed by the AIK. As described in Section 2.2, a counter-party can assess the status of an attesting party on basis of the PCR values in comparison with the SML. Inclusion of the two random values in the quote protects the communication from replay and man-in-the-middle attacks. Furthermore, all created random values must be stored in the SML and verified by a counter-party.

Processing of Step 3 is bound to a successful assessment of the communication partner. When a counter-party has provided evidence of a trusted state, a TrustMANET-Link is established and data can be transmitted without performing the whole handshake again. The previously exchanged shared secret is applied during encryption of data. It allows for protection of the payload and the symmetric key R from unintended access. Independent from the payload transmission, permanent sending and receiving of routing data (using TMC messages) is performed in the network. Confidentiality of OGMs is assured by an encryption algorithm. Only successfully assessed neighbours of a single node are able to decrypt OGMs using the received symmetric key R^i of the sender. The encryption ensures that it must origin from the possessors of the key R^i. It is authentic within the group of assessed neighbours.

It should be noted that the binding of the secrets S_{pub}^A and S_{pub}^B is not directly impled by the inclusion in the quote signature of the TPM. It requires the additional assumption that the software running on the node does behave correctly, i.e. does not include data coming from other nodes into quote messages or transfers secret keying information to other nodes. However, the quote signature is used to check that the correct software is running on the node and frequent re-attestation would show changes at runtime.

4.3   Routing Messages

The routing protocol consists of the three previously described messages. A distinguishing message type (MType) allows nodes to properly process them. None of the messages are relayed in the network as they have been received. Instead, TrustMANET-Messages incorporate payload and routing information. They have to be created on each hop of the route to a destination. According to the previously introduced protocol (see Table 1), the three message types TMC, TMQ and TMD have to be distinguished. TMDs carry payload, TMQs carry attestation information and TMCs carry a random number as well as the OGM message.

4.4   Routing Tables

Each node of the MANET maintains a routing table (see Table 2), containing connection details of all nodes of the network. Each entry of the table represents

Table 1. TrustMANET Handshake

0. Preconditions: Device set-up prior to operations.
$A:\qquad AIK_{priv}^A, AIKCert_{issuer}^B$
$B:\qquad AIK_{priv}^B, AIKCert_{issuer}^A$
1. TMC (Calls): Asynchronous broadcast transmission.
$A \rightarrow B:\qquad S_{pub}^A, enc\{OGM\}_{RA}$
$B \rightarrow A:\qquad S_{pub}^B, enc\{OGM\}_{RB}$
2. TMQ (Quote): Asynchronous unicast transmission.
$A \rightarrow B:\qquad Quote(S_{pub}^A, S_{pub}^B, PCR_{o..n})_{AIK_{priv}^A}, SML^A$
$B \rightarrow A:\qquad Quote(S_{pub}^B, S_{pub}^A, PCR_{o..n})_{AIK_{priv}^B}, SML^B$
3. TMD (Data): Asynchronous unicast transmission.
$A \rightarrow B:\qquad enc\left\{data := \{payload \parallel R^A\}\right\}_{SAB}$
$B \rightarrow A:\qquad enc\left\{data := \{payload \parallel R^B\}\right\}_{SAB}$

the best connection to a destination node. Best connections are described by a peer identifier (Next), indicating the next hop on the route, and the overall Metric. Nodes are addressed using their unique (but in-secure) *Media-Access-Control* (MAC) addresses, but securely identified using the AIKs. If a trustworthy connection to a neighbor could be established, the resulting shared secrets (S-Key and R-Key) is added to the table. Furthermore, each entry holds a public key (TPM-Key) which is required during the attestation process.

Table 2. Routing Table of node D

MAC	TPM-Key	S-Key	R-Key	Next	Metric
MAC_A	AIK_{pub}^A	n.n.	n.n.	B	m^A
MAC_B	AIK_{pub}^B	S^{BD}	R^B	B	m^B
MAC_C	AIK_{pub}^C	S^{CD}	R^C	C	m^C
MAC_D	AIK_{pub}^D	n.n.	R^D	D	m^D
MAC_E	AIK_{pub}^E	S^{ED}	R^E	E	m^E
MAC_M	AIK_{pub}^M	n.n.	n.n.	n.n.	n.n.

Figure 2 depicts an example topology of the described MANET including all relevant actors. In accordance with Table 2, D is directly connected to B, C, and E. A transmits OGMs (1, 2, 3) in the network and malicious node M is excluded from participation. Node D, which is in the transmission range of M, will not re any of its messages (4) until M provides the adequate proof of integrity. F   a designated node serving as gateway to other kinds of networks. If no certifi   .on for AIKs is used, MAC-Addresses and TPM-Keys are known in advanc   o all nodes, but the availability of S-Keys, R-Keys, Next-Nodes and Metr'   /alues depends on the respective topology. They might not be known (n.n.), y   S-Keys and R-Keys are only established between neighbors. The routing inf   .ation of trustworthy nodes will be forwarded in the network. Untrustwort'   .odes, e.g. malicious nodes or nodes running on deprecated software, can onl;   mmunicate to neighbors. They are not visible throughout the network, thu'   .cluded from the closed user group.

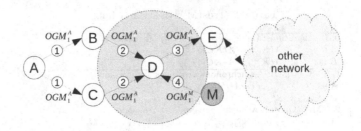

Fig. 2. Example Topology

4.5 Call Tables

Nodes frequently broadcast TMC messages, containing a random value (S-Key), within the transmission range of the sending device. The high frequency of TMC broadcasts increases the connectivity within dynamically changing topologies. This however, is limited to the capabilities of the underlying hardware, especially for the purpose of random number generating. In order to cope with this issue, random values should be reused in successive TMCs. After a certain period of time they become invalid. This approach might cause synchronization problems if e.g. the response is not delivered in time. For this reason, a certain amount of locally issued random values are kept in memory (see Table 3) of each device. Received random values of counter-parties are kept in memory, too. They expire according to the time of reception.

Table 3. Call Tables of Node A

Issued			Received		
S-Key	Validity	Expiry	S-Key	Validity	Expiry
$S0_{pub}^A$	delete	t_0	$S0_{pub}^B$	delete	t_0
$S1_{pub}^A$	expired	t_1	$S1_{pub}^B$	expired	t_1
$S2_{pub}^A$	valid	t_2	$S2_{pub}^B$	valid	t_2

Each node operates a sender and a receiver. Senders permanently broadcast S-Keys and receivers wait for incoming TMC messages. Figure 3 depicts the state diagram of Receiver A. Proceeding from the initial Wait, only the reception of a quote or a S-Key is accepted. Reception of an S-Key immediately leads to creation and sending of the first quote (Q1). Hereby, the current local S-Key (SA) is applied. After sending of Q, the receiver has to wait for the counter-party's quote.

When a quote comes in, the receiver has to verify whether SB is known. If SB is not known, e.g. lost during transmission, the quote can not be processed. It is rejected and the receiver has to wait again. An acceptable SB leads to a check of SA. Invalid SA (e.g. outdated) are rejected and the receiver starts waiting again. Once the SA is accepted, either the second Q must be sent or it is already sent. Both cases lead, as far as the attestation is successful, to

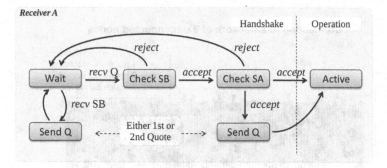

Fig. 3. State-Diagram of Receiver

an `Active` node that is ready for operation within the TrustMANET. Active nodes are connected to at least one other node of the MANET. They receive protected routing updates (TMC) and payload data (TMD) according to the protocol described in Section 4.2.

5   Measurements

The triggering of TPM calculations is handled by the user space daemon (`TrustMANET-Daemon / Management`) communicating and passing the needed data between the kernel module (`TrustMANET-Module`) and the TPM device. The Implementation was tested on a *Genuine Intel(R) CPU N270, 1,60GHz* with *2GB* of *RAM* with the Linux kernel version *3.0.0-14 (32-bit OS)* and an *Infineon TPM 1.2 4bit GPIO*. The experimental environment consists of three nodes (1,2,3) physically connected over a 100MBit network switch. Measurements were +made with a four node (defined to be the (ad-hoc) *supplicant*) +joining this network, as shown in Figure 4.

Note that these measurements include TPM calculations and the bilateral agreement of the supplicant and its counterpart.

The TPM is single threaded. Thus node 2 must wait for all TPM operations required for the attestation with node 1 to complete before it can attest. Similarly, node 3 must wait until all TPM operations for nodes 1 and 2 are complete. Looking deeper into the individual operations explains the average connection time of the supplicant to a single node of around 3.5 seconds as well as the additional time needed for the other nodes. Figure 5 shows the calculation time needed for the TPM quote and the time of verification. As given by the vendor, the TPM quote calculation is stated to be around 500 milliseconds. However, on the hardware used, longer times were measured. Thus, these times may vary on different TPM chips. it does however point out that the expensive calculations performed by the TPM are the bottleneck of the protocol.

While verification of a TPM quote consumes on average about 12.4 ms, the TPM quote generation is the most expensive operation in the whole communication process, taking on average 1604 ms. Nearly any other operations are

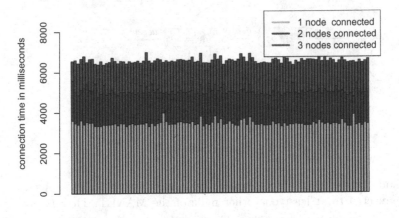

Fig. 4. Supplicant joining a network of 3 nodes

implemented concurrently, so that even when the TPM quote operation is executed, any other operation in the system not using the TPM can react and is not blocked. To improve the performance of the proposed protocol it is obviously mandatory to improve the performance of the TPM quote operation. It is shown that our extended BATMAN protocol is less influenced by the developed software modules but more by the cooperating TPM hardware device.

6   Conclusion and Outlook

This paper shows that hardware-based security can provide a workable solution to essential security issues of Mobile-Ad-Hoc Networks. The proposed protocol establishes trust-relationships on the link-layer of the network. The Trusted Platform Module serves as a root of trust. This enables devices to mutually attest the system states of each node in the network. This attestation is performed while joining the network and further allows the establish of protected channels for routing and payload data.

Especially the *trust-model* and the assumed transitivity of trust in the MANET, as well as a proper security validation, are subjects for future work. A concrete trust-model however, depends on requirements of the real application environment. Devices may attest installed software packages, executable binaries, memory areas, cryptographic keys, routing tables, etc. Systems appraising an attestation need to be provided with all necessary information to perform the appraisal (e.g. policies or white lists of expected measurements). If such information cannot be stored in advance, additional concepts are needed.

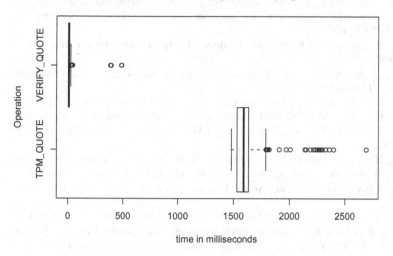

Fig. 5. Generating and verifying the TPM quote

Furthermore, *interoperability* to other networks standards, such as ISDN, GSM, UMTS or LTE, is of importance. It needs to be considered how Trust-MANET devices can interact with networks of the same kind or different types of devices, building a heterogeneous seamless communication system. Gateways are already part of the TrustMANET, however it has not yet been evaluated how a trustworthy connection can be maintained over another layer-2 protocol. In such scenarios, a gateway should not be implemented as the single point of failure.

A lot more issues must be placed under examination not only in other operative scenarios (e.g. forming groups) but also within the protocol and its architecture (e.g. group keys or anonymity and privacy). Also, the first measurements presented in section 5 and the prototype implementation must be extended. Empirical studies should reveal important characteristics, such as *performance* or *throughput* in several scenarios. Especially the TPM hardware device and its integration must be addressed to improve the performance of authentication. More recent experiments do show improvements in these aspects. Further, it needs to be questioned whether additional concepts are needed to achieve a network that is *scalable* and capable of delivering the intended services. Valuable related work was already provided by [16]. A general attestation mechanism is required in order to cope with more than one attesting and appraising application. Nevertheless, the first measurements showed a promising stable protocol, which covers several security issues of today's MANETs.

References

1. Brickell, E., Camenisch, J., Chen, L.: Direct anonymous attestation. In: Proceedings of the 11th ACM Conference on Computer and Communications Security, pp. 132–145. ACM (2004)
2. Carvalho, M.: Security in mobile ad hoc networks. IEEE Security & Privacy 6(2), 72–75 (2008)
3. Diffie, W., Hellman, M.: New directions in cryptography. IEEE Transactions on Information Theory 22(6), 644–654 (1976)
4. Garg, N., Mahapatra, R.P.: Manet security issues. IJCSNS 9(8), 241 (2009)
5. Goldman, K., Perez, R., Sailer, R.: Linking remote attestation to secure tunnel endpoints. In: Proceedings of the First ACM Workshop on Scalable Trusted Computing (2006)
6. Ikeda, M., Kulla, E., Hiyama, M., Barolli, L., Takizawa, M.: Experimental results of a manet testbed in indoor stairs environment. In: 2011 IEEE International Conference on Advanced Information Networking and Applications, pp. 779–786. IEEE (2011)
7. Kannhavong, B., Nakayama, H., Nemoto, Y., Kato, N., Jamalipour, A.: A survey of routing attacks in mobile ad hoc networks. Wireless Communication 14(5) (2007)
8. Kidston, D., Li, L., Tang, H., Mason, P.: Mitigating security threats in tactical networks. In: IST Panel Symposium, Military Communication and Networks, Wroclaw, Poland (2010)
9. Krishna Kishore, G., Sambasiva Rao, K.V.: An efficient trusted computing base for routing in MANETs. International Journal of Computer Science and Information Technologies 2(5) (2011)
10. Kuntze, N., Rudolph, C., Fuchs, A.: Trust in Peer-to-Peer Content Distribution Protocols. In: Samarati, P., Tunstall, M., Posegga, J., Markantonakis, K., Sauveron, D. (eds.) WISTP 2010. LNCS, vol. 6033, pp. 76–89. Springer, Heidelberg (2010)
11. Mazhar, N., Farooq, M.: BeeAIS: Artificial Immune System Security for Nature Inspired, MANET Routing Protocol, BeeAdHoc. In: de Castro, L.N., Von Zuben, F.J., Knidel, H. (eds.) ICARIS 2007. LNCS, vol. 4628, pp. 370–381. Springer, Heidelberg (2007)
12. Michiardi, P., Molva, R.: Simulation-based analysis of security exposures in mobile ad hoc networks. In: European Wireless Conference, Citeseer (2002)
13. Mitchell, C.: Trusted computing, vol. 6. Iet (2005)
14. Neumann, A., Aichele, C., Lindner, M., Wunderlich, S.: Better approach to mobile ad-hoc networking (B.A.T.M.A.N.) (2008)
15. SourceForge.net. Integrity measurement architecture (ima), http://sourceforge.net/projects/linux-ima
16. Stumpf, F., Fuchs, A., Katzenbeisser, S., Eckert, C.: Improving the scalability of platform attestation. In: Proceedings of the Third ACM Workshop on Scalable Trusted Computing (ACM STC 2008), 31 October, pp. 1–10. ACM Press, Fairfax (2008)
17. Tang, H., Salmanian, M.: Lightweight integrated authentication for tactical manets. In: ICYCS, pp. 2266–2271 (2008)
18. Trusted Computing Group. TPM 1.2 Main Specification (2011), http://www.trustedcomputinggroup.org/resources/tpm_main_specification
19. Xu, G., Borcea, C., Iftode, L.: A policy enforcing mechanism for trusted ad hoc networks. IEEE Transactions on Dependable and Secure Computing 8(3) (2011)

Panel Discussion: Mobile Device Trust — How Do We Link Social Needs, Technical Requirements, Techniques and Standards?

Shin'ichiro Matsuo

National Institute of Information and Communications Technology (NICT), Japan

Security and privacy issues on mobile device are the hottest issues in both research and industrial area. The prime issue in this topic is lack of trust model and links among social needs, technical requirements, realizing techniques, and technology standards. Constructing links among them is needed to build trust for mobile computing environment. Fig. 1 shows the relationship among these factors.

Social Needs is security and privacy needs in using mobile devices. Examples of the social needs are protecting personal information, transactions and action history. They are not depend on the architecture of mobile device and network system. Some of them are regulated by law and official guidelines, however, most of them are not clearly defined. The social needs are also changed by progress of technologies. For example, risk of tracking one's life-log is amplified by mobile-computing and cloud-computing. We must define the social needs with considering state-of-the-art technology.

Most of all security privacy issues are resulted from inefficient or malicious implementation of applications. These applications are executed in the smartphone and tablets. Here, they are represented as **Products**. The actual problem is mismatch between the social needs and product design and implementation. When we design and implement a software, we define the **Technical Requirements** on security and privacy. These requirements are output from standard information security management system [1] and risk evaluation framework [2]. This process is conducted with taking the network and computing **Environment** into account. At this time, we have no well-defined technical requirements, because the social needs are not defined and mobile device environment is still under developing. Here, we must study on the common technical requirement which fulfills the social needs.

Of course, **Realizing Techniques** are fundamental to build secure and privacy preserving mobile device. We already have many security techniques including cryptographic algorithms, cryptographic protocols, secure hardwares, sandboxing, virus protection techniques, privilege management and so on. Most of them are developed for PC and servers, and not enough for mobile devices. For example, mobile devices do not have enough capability to execute all function of PKI and light-weight authentication technologies are expected for mobile device. Thus, we must revisit further research directions to fulfill technical requirements which are specific for mobile devices.

Technology Standard is prime tool for deployment of these techniques. Most hardware and software products are designed and implemented in keeping with technology standards. For example, many cryptographic techniques are

C.J. Mitchell and A. Tomlinson (Eds.): INTRUST 2012, LNCS 7711, pp. 63–64, 2012.
© Springer-Verlag Berlin Heidelberg 2012

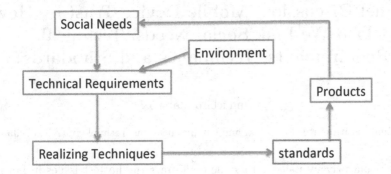

Fig. 1. Relationship among factors to build trust for mobile devices

standardized in ISO/IEC SC27/WG2 [3], specifications on trusted platform module are standardized in TCG [4], and many secure protocols are standardized in IETF [5]. Enhancing activities of standardizing organizations are indispensable to build a trust for mobile device.

The "trust" for mobile device can be established from building well-defined components for all above factors. Then we must construct links and chains among them. The chain itself will become the trust for the mobile device. In this panel session, we discuss on issues and further directions to build well-defined components and construct such links.

References

1. ISO/IEC 27001: Information technology Security techniques Information security management systems - Requirements (2005)
2. ISO/IEC 15408-1: Information technology – Security techniques – Evaluation criteria for IT security – Part 1: Introduction and general model (2009)
3. ISO/IEC JTC1 SC27/WG2,
   http://www.iso.org/iso/iso_technical_committee?commid=45306
4. Trusted Computing Group, http://www.trustedcomputinggroup.org/
5. Internet Engineering Task Force, Security Area,
   http://trac.tools.ietf.org/area/sec/trac/wiki

Security in the Distributed Internet of Things

Rodrigo Roman[1] and Javier Lopez[2]

[1] Institute for Infocomm Research, Singapore
rroman@i2r.a-star.edu.sg
[2] University of Malaga, Spain
jlm@lcc.uma.es

1   Summary

In the Internet of Things (IoT) [1], services can be provisioned using centralized architectures (central entities acquiring, processing, and providing information), but various types of distributed architectures can be used as well [2]. The foundations of these distributed architectures are the "edge intelligence" principle (the location of the intelligence and the provisioning of services at the edge of the network) and the "collaboration" principle (the collaboration between diverse entities in order to achieve a common goal). In fact, these two principles are core elements in the construction of 'decentralized systems' [3] and 'distributed systems' [4], respectively.

Following these two principles, we can classify the distributed architectures into three types: *Collaborative IoT* (various central entities exchange data and/or information with each other), *Connected Intranets of Things* (data acquisition networks not only process local information, but also provide it to both central entities and local/remote users), and *Distributed IoT* (all entities can have the ability to retrieve, process, combine, and provide information and services to other entities).

All these architectures have their own advantages and disadvantages. As Centralized IoTs make use of cloud infrastructures to provide a single data acquisition API for all devices, not only it is easy to integrate new devices into the system, but also the overall availability of the system is very high. Collaborative IoTs and Connected Intranets of Things require of additional interoperability mechanisms, but the scalability and robustness of the system is greatly improved. Finally, the Distributed IoT approach combines most of the advantages and disadvantages of the previous two approaches (superior scalability and robustness, infrastructure complexity), and also allows users and data acquisition networks to better manage their own data.

However, all aforementioned architectures share one common challenge: security. Although it is nearly impossible that an attacker can control the whole IoT, there are various threats that can affect the IoT services, such as physical damage, denial of service (DoS), eavesdropping/extracting information, and controlling a subset of the system [5]. In fact, no architecture is better than the other in terms of threats. In a centralized architecture, the central entity becomes a single point of failure, but the number of attack vectors are smaller.

C.J. Mitchell and A. Tomlinson (Eds.): INTRUST 2012, LNCS 7711, pp. 65–66, 2012.
© Springer-Verlag Berlin Heidelberg 2012

Distributed architectures are the exact opposite case: the impact from attacks is lessened, but there are more attack vectors. Therefore, all architectures need of various security mechanisms, such as protocol and network security, identity management, privacy, trust and governance, and fault tolerance [6].

In distributed architectures, it is more complex to solve the previously mentioned security challenges. As all entities are able to acquire and process information from other sources, some kind of authentication logic must be integrated into every 'thing'. Regarding access control, it is necessary to deal not only with the management of heterogeneous policies and permissions, but also with specific policy elements such as granularity (i.e. providing more details to people with the right credentials) and location (i.e. checking whether users are accessing the services of a thing locally or remotely). The implementation of security protocols and the management of credentials must also be seriously considered, since constrained entities can connect with other previously unknown entities at any time. Finally, it is necessary to create a good infrastructure for exchanging critical information about the state of the system.

On the other hand, the distributed approach is inherently more privacy-friendly, as the entities controlled directly by the users can make more decisions regarding the data they manage. The main benefits are as follows: i) entities can control the granularity of the data they produce, ii) entities can define their own access policies, and iii) entities do not need to provide all the data they produce, only the data that is needed by the external entities for a particular service. Moreover, distributed IoT entities can collaborate with centralized IoT entities so as to improve the trust management and overall fault tolerance of the whole system. For example, entities located at the edge of the network can provide detailed system status information (e.g. network status, existing connections between entities). This information can be used not only to pinpoint problematic data flows, but also to discover entities that can provide a reliable service in case of system failure.

References

1. CERP-IoT Cluster: Visions and Challenges for Realising the Internet of Things. European Commission (2010)
2. IoT-A project - Internet of Things Architecture (accessed on September, 2012)
3. Jones, G.: Organizational Theory, Design, and Change, 7th edn. Prentice Hall (2012)
4. Tanenbaum, A., van Steen, M.: Distributed Systems: Principles and Paradigms. Prentice Hall (2002)
5. Babar, S., Mahalle, P., Stango, A., Prasad, N., Prasad, R.: Proposed security model and threat taxonomy for the internet of things (IoT). In: Meghanathan, N., Boumerdassi, S., Chaki, N., Nagamalai, D. (eds.) CNSA 2010. CCIS, vol. 89, pp. 420–429. Springer, Heidelberg (2010)
6. Roman, R., Najera, P., Lopez, J.: Securing the Internet of Things. IEEE Computer 44, 51–58 (2011)

A Multi-criteria-Based Evaluation of Android Applications*

Gianluca Dini[1], Fabio Martinelli[2], Ilaria Matteucci[2], Marinella Petrocchi[2],
Andrea Saracino[1,2], and Daniele Sgandurra[2]

[1] Dipartimento di Ingegneria dell' Informazione, Università di Pisa, Italy
name.surname@iet.unipi.it
[2] Istituto di Informatica e Telematica, CNR, Pisa, Italy
name.surname@iit.cnr.it

Abstract. Android users can face the risk of downloading and installing bad applications on their devices. In fact, many applications may either hide malware, or their expected behavior do not fully follow the user's expectation. This happens because, at install-time, even if the user is warned with the potential security threat of the application, she often skips this alert message. On Android this is due to the complexity of the permission system, which may be tricky to fully understand.

We propose a multi-criteria evaluation of Android applications, to help the user to easily understand the trustworthiness degree of an application, both from a security and a functional side. We validate our approach by testing it on more than 180 real applications found either on official and unofficial markets.

1 Introduction

Android is an open source Operative System (OS) designed for mobile devices, such as smartphones and tablets, that currently has the largest share of the mobile device market. Part of its success is due to the large number of applications (or *apps*) that are available for Android devices, which can be developed using the Standard Development Kit (SDK). Android SDK is free to download and to use: hence, virtually anyone can develop applications, from expert and professional developers to programmers with limited experience. Applications are distributed through the application market, in which any user (even malicious ones) can share their own applications. The greatest channel for application distribution is *Google Play* (formerly known as *Android Market*), which tries to ensure the quality of distributed apps with some simple control mechanisms. However, it is always possible to get into low-quality applications, or malicious ones, when surfing Android markets or the several unofficial markets found on the web, especially if we consider that in these unofficial markets applications can be distributed without any kind of control.

Malicious applications are the greatest security threat for Android systems and, hence, to prevent such applications to damage smartphones, Android implements two

---

* The research leading to these results has received funding from the European Union Seventh Framework Programme (FP7/2007-2013) under grant no 256980 (NESSoS) and under grant no 257930 (Aniketos).

C.J. Mitchell and A. Tomlinson (Eds.): INTRUST 2012, LNCS 7711, pp. 67–82, 2012.
© Springer-Verlag Berlin Heidelberg 2012

security-control mechanisms: *sandboxing* and *permissions* [1]. *Sandboxing* is achieved by means of application isolation: each application runs in its own instance of the Dalvik Virtual Machine (DVM), an optimization of the Java Virtual Machine, and each DVM is treated as a different UNIX user, by the Android's underlying Linux kernel. The isolation ensures that malicious applications do not interfere with the activity of the good ones. The *permission* system is a mechanism of access control to protect resources and critical operations. At install-time, permissions required by an application are shown to the user, which can decide whether to grant or to deny them. However, several criticisms have been raised against this system, which results too coarse-grained [2] and too much reliant on user knowledge and expertise [3]. The main problem of this approach is that the acceptance policy for an application's requested permission is "all or nothing", that is, the user cannot accept only a subset of the required permissions. Then, if the user does not agree even with a single permission, the installation is not performed. Furthermore, due to the large number of existing permissions, even an expert user may not fully understand all of them and, as a consequence, several users install applications without caring about the required permissions and without questioning about the potential security threats [3]. Hence, a simpler mechanism to guide average users in the job of deciding whether to install or not an application is necessary, without the burden of reading (and understanding) all the declared permissions.

In this paper we present a multi-criteria approach that combines information retrieved from permissions with the reputation indexes provided by markets, to compute the trustworthiness of an application and the security threat that it may represent. In more detail, the contribution of the paper are the following:

- we propose a novel classification of Android permissions, in which we assign to each permission a *threat score* according to the criticality of both resources and critical operations they control;
- we compute a *global threat score* for each application, which is a function of the threat score of all the required permissions;
- we propose the application of the Analytical Hierarchy Process (AHP), a well-known methodology for multi-criteria decision, to classify applications according to the global threat score and to reputation indexes retrievable from markets. Each application can be considered *trusted*, or *untrusted*, or *deceptive*. By following the suggested value of the classification, users can avoid the installation of potentially infected or not-properly behaving applications;
- we validate our approach applying the methodology to 180 real applications with different features, where 40 applications were infected by common malware. The tested applications have been correctly classified. Hence, the user can consider the trustworthiness level of the application by only observing the result of this classification process, without the need of understanding all of the requested permissions.

The paper is organized as follows: in Section 2, we explain how we classify permissions and how we measure the threat of applications. Section 3 recalls the AHP methodology and how it is applied in our scenario. Section 4 reports the results of our approach and some practical examples. Section 5 points to some related work concerning the Android permission system. Finally, Section 6 briefly concludes, proposing some future extensions.

2 Classification of Android Permissions

In this section we give some notions on the Android permission system and we explain how we assign a threat score to each permission and a global threat score to an application.

Currently, Android defines 120 permissions[1], where each permission is related to a specific device resource or to a critical operation that can possibly be exploited to harm the user privacy, her money, or the device itself. Permissions required by an application are declared in the AndroidManifest.xml file that is part of the application itself and that is bound to it by means of digital signature.

Android classifies permissions in four classes: *normal, dangerous, signature*, and *signature-or-system*. For the scope of this paper, we focus on the first two classes. In fact, *signature* and *signature-or-system* Android permissions cannot be required by custom applications, since only applications signed with the Google private key can use those permissions. The Android permission classification is used to choose which permissions have to be shown to the user at install-time. The *dangerous* permissions are automatically shown to the user, whereas the *normal* ones are listed in a separate sublist addressed as "Other Permissions". If the user accepts all the permissions required by an application, then this application is installed and, at run-time, it is allowed to use the critical resources and operations granted to the permissions without asking for further authorizations.

Several criticisms have been raised against the Android permission system. Firstly, the system is too coarse-grained [2], since the user can only choose whether to accept all of the permissions declared by an application or to refuse to install the application. Furthermore, the user is usually unable to determine if an application can be trusted, based upon this list of required permissions. In fact, there are several permissions and some of them are really difficult to understand even to expert users. It is often the case that average users do not care about permissions and their security hazards, thus installing potentially malicious applications [3]. Furthermore, some developers are used to declare more permissions in the manifest file than those effectively needed by the application (the so called *Permission Overdeclaration* [4]). This happens because some permissions have similar names and their description is not self-explicative for some developers. Therefore, Android users, seeing a very long permission list when installing a new application, are less encouraged to read and understand them.

To overcome the problem of permission understanding, we discuss a novel way to compute the threat score of an application, based upon the requested permissions. The proposed system shows to the user, in a simple way, the dangerousness of the application. This score is a number ranging over the interval $[0, 15]$, where 0 represents an application that only requires unharmful permissions, whilst 15 is a strongly critical application that requires all the Android permissions.

---

[1] http://developer.android.com/reference/android/Manifest.permission.html

2.1 Threat Indexes

The goal of the proposed method is to compute a threat score of applications according to the permissions that they declare. For this reason, we have analysed all the 120 default Android permissions, and scored according to their threat. For each permission we have defined three threat indexes, to represent the type of threat and the severity of damage that can be achieved if these permissions are exploited by a malicious application. These indexes are: *privacy* threat, *system* threat, and *money* threat, and they are defined in the interval $[0, 1]$, where 0 means no threat and 1 means the highest threat (see Table 1). We have assigned to each permission these three threat values, according to the actions, or resources, controlled by that specific permission and their relation with well-known malware attacks. In more details, the rationale of which value to assign to each threat index, according to the considered permission, is discussed in the following.

Table 1. Threat Levels

0	No Threat
0.2	Low Threat
0.4	Low-to-Moderate Threat
0.6	Moderate Threat
0.8	Moderate-to-High Threat
1	High Threat

Privacy Threat. Permissions with a high value of this threat are those that control the access to sensitive data, e.g. the user's contact list, stored files, Internet bookmarks and chronology, or SIM and device information such as the IMEI and IMSI codes. On the other hand, a medium-low value of privacy threat is assigned to those permissions that access sensors such as camera or microphone, since they can be maliciously used to spy the user behavior.

System Threat. A high value of system threat is assigned to applications accessing system data, e.g. permissions that allows the application to write to the device memory, install and uninstall other applications, or access sensors whose improper use can leak the battery energy.

Money Threat. High values of this index are assigned to permissions that control services whose use directly imply a money cost, such a phone calls or outgoing SMS. Conversely, if the cost is indirectly related to a specific permission, it receives a medium money threat value, e.g. the CHANGE_NETWORK_STATE permission that allows an application to enable or disable the data connection whose available traffic amount is generally limited to a few Gigabytes per month and, afterward, the user has to pay all the outgoing/incoming traffic byte per byte.

Example. The permission SEND_SMS enables an application to send SMS messages without requiring user confirmation. Thus, an application that declares this permission can send SMS messages, with any text, at any rate, and at any phone number, without the user noticing it (unless she checks her available credit). This permission has been exploited by several malware to leak the user credit by sending messages to premium-rate number, or to threaten her privacy by sending information, such as the IMEI and IMSI codes, to a phone number controlled by the attacker [5]. Table 2 shows the threat indexes assigned to the permission SEND_SMS.

Table 2. Threat Level of SEND_SMS permission

Permission	Privacy Threat	System Threat	Money Threat
SEND_SMS	0.8	0	1

The privacy threat is considered medium-high since SMS messages can be used as a vector to steal sensitive information (some malware use them to do so). However, this information has to be accessed before it can be sent and this requires other specific permissions. Our complete classification of Android permissions can be found in [6]. It is worth noticing that we do not consider the default "signature" and "signature-or-system" permissions, since they can only be requested by device manufactures or by Google applications that we assume trustworthy. Moreover, those permissions are not shown to the user at install-time, thus they should not be part of the scoring process.

2.2 Global Threat Score

For each application α, we define the *global threat score* σ, which is a function of the threat score of all the permissions declared by the application α, as follows:

$$\sigma = \frac{\sum_{i=1}^{n} w_p pt_i + w_s st_i + w_m mt_i}{max\left\{1, \lceil log(n) \rceil \right\}} \quad (1)$$

where n is the number of permissions declared by the application α, pt_i, st_i, mt_i are, respectively, the privacy, system, and money threat of the i-th permission required by α, and w_p, w_t, w_m are used to weight the importance of a specific threat factor. In the current implementation, we consider w_m being three times greater than w_t and w_p: we consider the money threat the more relevant, since it can harm the user more directly. The number of permissions that concern privacy threat and system threat are three time larger than the number of permissions concerning money. The denominator of (1) should render the idea that an application with a lot of medium threat permissions should not be considered as dangerous as an application that comes with few extremely dangerous permissions. However, since the increase of the denominator is logarithmic, it is not feasible for an attacker to hide the threat of an application declaring a large number of low threat permissions. We consider applications with σ lower than 4 as *low-threat* applications, while ones with σ in the interval $[4, 7]$ are *moderate threat* to *high-threat*. Higher values of σ mean *extremely* critical applications.

The value σ estimates how much an application is critical from the security point of view. Hence, the more permissions are required by an application, and the more dangerous these permissions are, the more critical the application becomes. If an application receives a low-threat score, this should increase the likelihood that this application is downloaded and, as a consequence, this should encourage developers to accurately choose the permissions required by their applications. However, several applications actually require a large number of permissions to perform all their functions, especially *communication* and *social* applications, and they should not be considered as suspicious. This leads us to rely on a multi-criteria decision system (Section 3) in order to classify an application with respect to a set of criteria, among which the threat score σ.

3   Multi-criteria Assessment of Android Applications

In this section, we show how to apply the Analytical Hierarchy Process (AHP) to assess the security level of an Android application. Before instantiating the methodology, we briefly recall the basic steps of AHP.

3.1   The Analytical Hierarchy Process

The Analytic Hierarchy Process (AHP) [7,8] is a multi-criteria decision making technique, which has been largely used in several fields of study. Given a decision problem, where several different *alternatives* can be chosen to reach a *goal*, AHP returns the *most relevant* alternative with respect to a set of previously established *criteria*. This approach requires to subdivide a complex problem into a set of sub-problems, equal in number to the chosen criteria, and then compute the solution (alternative) by properly merging the various local solutions for each sub-problem.

The process can be described using an example: let the reader suppose to have as *goal* "choosing a restaurant for dinner". The possible alternatives are a Japanese sushi bar, a French *brasserie*, and an Italian *trattoria*. The problem must be structured as a hierarchy, as shown in Figure 1, linking goal and alternatives through a set of criteria. In the proposed example, appropriate *criteria* could be: cost, food, and staff.

Once the hierarchy is built, the relevance of each alternative with respect to each criterion is established, comparing them in a pairwise fashion. Comparisons are done through a scale of numbers typical to AHP (see Table 3). The scale indicates how many

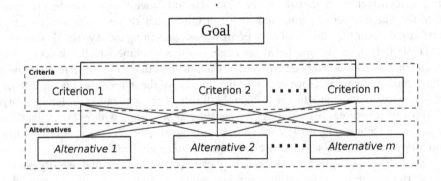

Fig. 1. Generic AHP Hierarchy

Table 3. Fundamental Scale for AHP

Intensity	Definition	Explanation
1	Equal	Two elements contribute equally to the objective
3	Moderate	One element is slightly more relevant than another
5	Strong	One element is strongly more relevant over another
7	Very strong	One element is very strongly more relevant over another
9	Extreme	One element is extremely more relevant over another

times an alternative is *more relevant* than another one, with respect to a specific criterion. The relevance is established according either to subjective or objective statements; for example, if the Italian trattoria is much more cheaper than the Japanese sushi bar, we can state that the alternative trattoria is strongly more relevant (and then more advised) than the sushi bar according to the *cost* criterion.

Pairwise Comparison Matrices. Pairwise comparisons for each criterion are expressed in a matricial form, called *pairwise comparison matrices*. A pairwise comparisons matrix M is a square matrix $n \times n$ (where n is the number of *alternatives*), which has positive entries and it is reciprocal, i.e. for each element a_{ij}, $a_{ij} = \frac{1}{a_{ji}}$. For the comparisons matrices the concept of *consistence* is defined. A comparison matrix of size $n \times n$ is consistent if $a_{i,j} \cdot a_{j,k} = a_{i,k}$, $\forall(i,j,k)$. If a comparison matrix is consistent, the pairwise comparisons are well related between them. However, it is difficult to obtain perfectly consistent matrices using empirically defined comparisons. AHP requires that comparisons matrices are, at least, semi-consistent. To measure the consistency of a comparison matrix, the consistency index $CI = \frac{\lambda_{max} - n}{n-1}$ has been defined [9]. For a consistent matrix $CI = 0$, whilst a matrix is considered semi-consistent if $CI < 0.1$. If this condition does not hold, the comparisons matrix should be re-evaluated. Table 4 shows the comparison matrix for the *cost* criterion of the three restaurants example. The same procedure is repeated to compare the restaurants with respect to the other criteria, namely food and staff, obtaining two additional comparisons matrices that we do not report for the sake of brevity.

Table 4. Example Comparisons Matrix: Restaurants vs Cost (CI=0.0018473)

COST	Japanese	Italian	French	Loc. Prio.
Japanese	1	$\frac{1}{5}$	$\frac{1}{3}$	0.11
Italian	5	1	2	0.58
French	3	$\frac{1}{2}$	1	0.31

How to Compute Local Priorities. Local priorities express the relevance of the alternatives for a specific criterion. Given a comparison matrix, local priorities are computed as the normalized eigenvector associated with the largest eigenvalue [10]. In Table 4, the vector of local priorities for the cost criterion is reported on the right side of the matrix, and it expresses that, for the cost criterion, the Italian restaurant is the most advised among the three alternatives.

Furthermore, it is possible to express the relevance of a criterion with respect to the goal. For example, if the dinner cost has more relevance than the kindness of the staff, that is, we may accept that the staff kindness is not satisfactory, but is very important that the dinner is cheap, this can be specified using the scale of Table 3. Hence, we have an additional pairwise comparisons matrix for the criteria, which size is $k \times k$ where k is the number of criteria.

How to Compute Global Priorities. Global priorities are computed through a weighted sum of the local priorities computed in the previous step:

$$P_g^{a_i} = \sum_{j=1}^{k} p_g^{c_j} \cdot p_{c_j}^{a_i} \tag{2}$$

where $P_g^{a_i}$ is the global priority of the alternative a_i, $p_g^{c_j}$ is the local priority of criterion c_j with respect to goal and $p_{c_j}^{a_i}$ is the local priority of alternative a_i with respect to criterion c_j. The vector of global priorities for the restaurant problem is computed as:

$$P_g = 0.47 \begin{bmatrix} 0.11 \\ 0.58 \\ 0.31 \end{bmatrix} + 0.15 \begin{bmatrix} 0.1 \\ 0.6 \\ 0.3 \end{bmatrix} + 0.38 \begin{bmatrix} 0.31 \\ 0.24 \\ 0.45 \end{bmatrix} = \begin{bmatrix} 0.19 \\ 0.45 \\ 0.36 \end{bmatrix}$$

Where $\{0.47, 0.15, 0.38\}$ are an example of local priorities of the criteria, and the column vectors are the local priorities of each criterion w.r.t. the three alternatives. This result means that the Italian trattoria is the best choice[2].

3.2 An AHP Instance for Evaluating Android Applications

We instantiate the AHP decision methodology to assess the quality of an Android application as follows: given an Android application with the following parameters: a threat score σ, a developer δ, a number of download η, a market μ, a user-rating ρ, then the *goal* consists in assigning to the application one the following *alternative* labels:

Trusted. This alternative means that the application correctly works and should not hide malicious functionalities.

Untrusted. This alternative means that, even if apparently working as the user expects from a functional perspective, the application could violate the security of the mobile device.

Deceptive. This alternative means that the application is neither functional nor secure.

---

[2] The numerical values have been assigned as an example to show a well-formed matrix. The authors do not aim at ranking Japanese, Italian, and French restaurants.

The problem is parametric w.r.t. the application, thus for two different applications the same fixed alternatives have a different relevance w.r.t. the same criterion. Hence, the five parameters (σ, δ, η, μ, ρ), wich are the *criteria* of the problem, assume different values for different applications.

In the following we explain how to build the related comparison matrices and the possible values that each criterion may assume:

Market (μ). Applications are generally distributed through application markets. The most popular market is Google Play, also referred as the *official* market. A developer that wants to publish applications on Google Play has to buy a developer account at the price of 25$, receiving in exchange a private key that she will use to digitally sign her application before publishing them [1]. If users report an application as malicious, then this application is removed both from the market and remotely from all the devices that have installed it; moreover, the developer can be tracked and blacklisted. In addition, Google Play includes some reputation indexes that should help the user to understand the application quality. These features make the official market a trustworthy place where to download apps. Nevertheless, several malware have been found in the Android Market [11][12] starting from the second half of year 2011.

There exists also a plethora of *unofficial* marketplaces that do not require developer registration and that give access to some applications that are not available on the market. However, unofficial markets often miss reputation indexes and sometimes there is no control on the quality of the applications, so that it is easier to accidentally download malicious applications. We also consider a third value for the market parameter: *manually installed*. This is the case in which the user manually installs the application, without the need of an installer, like those that are usually necessary to download apps from markets, both official and unofficial ones. With reference to Table 3, we show the *relevance* of each alternative, for the three possible values of μ:

- μ = official: we consider that *trusted* is moderately more relevant than *deceptive* and strongly more relevant than *untrusted*.
- μ = unofficial: we consider that *untrusted* is moderately more relevant than *trusted* and slightly more relevant than *deceptive*.
- μ = manually installed: we consider that *untrusted* is slightly more relevant than *trusted* and *deceptive* (that are equally relevant).

According to this information, comparison matrices (full list in [6]) are directly computed.

Developer (δ). We consider three types of developers: *standard*, *Top*, and *Google*. Google rewards the best developers with a *Top Developer* badge, reported on each application they publish. Hence, we are considering these developers as strongly trusted and known to produce high-quality applications. On Google Play, *Google Inc.* itself is considered a Top Developer; however, we consider Google more trusted than other developers, since it distributes apps that often are vital to the normal activity of Android smartphones.

All the other developers are considered standard and since the Top Developer badge is only used on Google Play, all the developers of applications from unofficial markets have been labeled standard. We make this assumption because applications coming from unofficial markets can be modified versions of well-known applications on Google Play, but these modifications also change the identity of the developer, together with her trustworthiness.

Evaluating pairs of alternatives with respect to the developer means that:

- δ = Google: we consider that *trusted* is extremely more relevant than *deceptive* and *untrusted* (that are equally relevant).
- δ = Top Developer: we consider that *trusted* is very strongly more relevant than *untrusted* and *deceptive* (that are equally relevant).
- δ = Standard: we consider that the three alternatives are equally relevant.

Number of Downloads (η). Several markets report the number of downloads for each application. As an example, the so-called "killer applications", i.e. extremely popular apps, have been downloaded from Google Play more than 100 millions of times. In our opinion, these applications should be considered differently from those downloaded much fewer time, e.g. less than 100 times. Hence, we define 7 intervals in which the value η may fall. For very high values of η, *trusted* is extremely relevant. As the value of η decreases, the relevance slowly passes from *trusted* to *untrusted*.

User Rating (ρ). Users can rate applications and leave a comment, which can be shown to other users. Rating is generally expressed as a number that ranges from 1 to 5. We consider applications with a rate less than 2 as *low-quality*, for which the *deceptive* alternative is extremely more relevant than the *trusted* one. A score higher than 4 means a *high-to-very-high* quality apps for which the *trusted* alternative is very strongly more relevant than the other two. Intermediate values mean a neutral comparisons matrix.

Threat Score (σ). For each application the threat score is computed as explained in Section. 2. We define the following intervals:

- $\sigma < 4$: *trusted* is very strongly more relevant than *untrusted* and moderately more relevant than *deceptive*.
- $4 \leq \sigma \leq 7$: *untrusted* is very strongly more relevant than the other alternatives (that are equally relevant).
- $\sigma > 7$: *untrusted* is extremely more relevant than *trusted*, and *deceptive* is strongly more relevant than *trusted*.

For marketplaces without download counters and/or rating systems, we define two additional comparison matrices whose elements are all equal to 1. Globally, we define 20 comparison matrices, but it is possible to increase their number to compute a finer granularity for each criterion. Finally, it is worth noticing that the list of proposed criteria is not exhaustive, and the methodology allows the insertion of other rules helpful to evaluate the alternatives. In the current implementation we consider all the criteria as equally relevant.

4   Implementation and Results

We have developed a framework to analyze and classify Android applications, which fully implements the previous strategy. Since several markets do not allow the direct download of apk files on a personal computer, and the applications are installed directly on the device through an installer, we have firstly used the ADB tool to extract the apk files from the device and, secondly, apktool decoder[3] to extract the manifest files.

To compute the application threat score σ, we have extracted the permissions from the manifest file using an XML parser, and we have computed its σ value according to formula (1). We have used Matlab[4] to implement AHP. Our test-set is composed of 180 Android applications of different categories, which we know in advance to be:

- *Good App*: Application that behaves correctly both from the security and functional point of view.
- *Infected*: Application infected by a malware.
- *Bad App*: Application whose behavior is not coherent with the declared one.

For each application, the five parameters (score σ, market μ, developer δ, rating ρ, and download number η) have been given as input to our implementation of AHP.

In more detail, the test-set consists of:

- 90 applications that come from Google Play, and 50 that come from unofficial markets, whilst 40 are manually installed. Two of the applications coming from unofficial markets and 38 of those manually installed are infected by malware.
- Application categories: Augmented Reality, Books and News, Communication, Desktop Manager, Entertainment, File Managing, Game, Social and Utility, and Antivirus.
- The applications user rating ranges over $\{1, \ldots, 5\}$.
- The number of downloads ranges over $[0, 10M+]$.
- Applications produced by standard developers, Top Developers, or Google.

The results of the tests are shown in Figure 2. All the infected applications have been recognized by AHP as *untrusted*. It is worth noticing that some good apps also fall in this class. These applications come from unofficial markets (labelled as Unoff. in the graph of Figure 2), for which no user rating was available and, hence, they cannot be considered trusted. However, if new information became available for these applications, they will eventually be considered as trusted ones. All the applications coming from Google Play have been classified either as *trusted* or *deceptive* on the base of the user rating, threat score, and number of downloads. All the bad apps applications have been considered *deceptive*.

In the following subsection we describe the application of AHP to two of these applications and the corresponding results.

4.1   Baseball Superstars 2010

Let us suppose that we are uncertain about the nature of an application called Baseball Superstars 2010. We can apply AHP using the values of the five parameters in Table 5. As an example, Table 6 shows the matrix used to compare the three alternatives with respect to the application developer criterion. Baseball Superstars 2010 has been developed by a *Top Developer*.

---

[3] http://code.google.com/p/android-apktool
[4] http://www.mathworks.com/products/matlab/

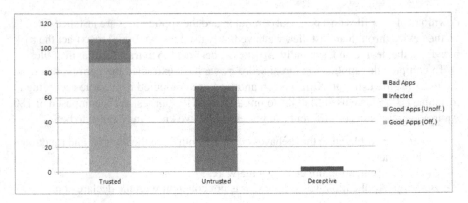

Fig. 2. Evaluation Results

Table 5. Parameters of Baseball Superstars 2010

Name	σ	ρ	μ	δ	η
BBSS2010	1	3.8	Google Play	Top Developer	10M+

Table 6. Alternatives vs Criterion: Developer for BBSS2010

top developer	Trusted	Untrusted	Deceptive	Loc.Prio.
Trusted	1	4	7	0.7
Untrusted	$\frac{1}{4}$	1	4	0.23
Deceptive	$\frac{1}{7}$	$\frac{1}{4}$	1	0.07

Top Developers generally produce high quality apps and they are not likely to publish malicious apps. This is supported by the priorities shown in Table 6. We notice that *trusted* is very strongly favored with respect to *deceptive* and strongly favored with respect to *untrusted*. *Trusted* obtains a higher priority with respect to the other alternatives. Using (2), we merge these local priorities with the ones coming from the comparison matrices for the other four parameters. Thus, we have the vector of the global priorities: $\{0.7, 0.16, 0.14\}$, meaning that the application is considered *trusted*

On a repository of well-known malicious apps[5], we have found an infected version of this game trojanized by the Geinimi malware. This malware leaks information concerning both the user and the device, which is sent via SMS to a number controlled by the attacker. Moreover, it opens a backdoor[6]. Table 7 shows the parameters' values for

---

[5] http://contagiominidump.blogspot.com

[6] http://www.symantec.com/security_response/writeup.jsp?
docid=2011-010111-5403-99&tabid=2

Table 7. Two Versions of Baseball Superstars 2010

Name	σ	ρ	μ	δ	η
BBSS2010	1	3.8	Google Play	Top Developer	10M+
BBSS2010 (Trojan)	7.3	-	-	Standard Developer	-

the two versions of the app. The trojanized version of Baseball Superstars asks several permissions; hence, its threat score σ is much higher than the genuine version. Applying AHP, we have the following global priorities for the malware: $\{0.23, 0.49, 0.28\}$. The potential danger of the application has been recognized; in fact, AHP classifies this application as *untrusted*.

4.2 Skype

Skype is a popular software used for VoIP and free chat and its mobile version obtained a large success: anyone can make phone calls via Skype with their smartphones, using the data connection instead of the classical and expensive phone call. To work properly, the Android version of Skype requires a large number of permissions with a high threat. In fact, computing the threat score with the expression presented in Section 2, Skype gets a score of 6.8. Therefore, Skype is an example of a high threat application. In our analysis, we have considered two Skype versions, as reported in Table 8.

Table 8. Two Skype Versions

Name	σ	ρ	μ	δ	η
Skype	6.8	3.8	Google Play	Standard Developer	10M+
Skype	6.8	4	Unofficial	Standard Developer	-

Applying AHP on the version of Skype coming from the official market, we have produced the following global priorities vector $\{0.47, 0.4, 0.13\}$, which means that the application looks *trusted*; in fact, the reputation of the market, and the large number of downloads, strongly raise the trustworthiness of this application, even if it has received a high threat score. For the Skype version downloaded from the unofficial market, which does not even provide a download counter, the global priorities are: $\{0.29, 0.52, 0.19\}$, and the application is considered *untrusted*. Even if the two versions of this app require the same set of permissions, it is possible that their source codes are different (possibly malicious). Since more than 10 millions of users have downloaded the version from the official market, it is strongly unlikely that malicious behaviors have not been noticed and reported, forcing the application removal from the market.

5 Related Work

Several extensions and improvements to the Android permissions system have been recently proposed. [13] proposes a security framework that regulates the actions of

Android applications defining security rules concerning permissions and sequence of operations. New rules can be added using a specification language. The application code is analyzed at deployment-time to verify whether it is compliant to the rule, otherwise it is considered as malicious code. Our proposal does not require the code to be decompiled and analyzed, since it only requires the permissions list that can be retrieved from the manifest file and other generic information that can be retrieved from the website where the application can be downloaded.

Authors of [2] present a finer grained model of the Android permission system. They propose a framework, named *TISSA*, that modifies the Android system to allow the user to choose the permissions she wants to grant to an application and those that have to be denied. Using data mocking, they ensure that an application works correctly even if it is not allowed to access the required information. However, their system focuses on the analysis of privacy threatening permissions and it relies on the user expertise and knowledge. A work similar to TISSA is presented in [14]. The authors designed an improved application installer that allows to define three different policies for each permission: allow, deny, or conditional allow. Conditional allow is used to define a customized policy for a specific permission by means of a policy definition language. However, the responsibility of choosing the right permissions still falls on the user.

In [15], applications have been classified on the base of their required permissions. Applications have been divided in functional clusters by means of Self Organizing Maps, proving that apps with the same set of permission have similar functionalities. However this work does not differentiate between good and bad (trojanized) apps. Finally, another analysis of Android permissions is presented in [4], where the authors discuss a tool, *Stowaway*, which discovers permission overdeclaration errors in apps. Using this tool, it is possible to analyze the 85% of Android available functions, including the private ones, to obtain a mapping between functions and permissions.

AHP has been used in several settings to make decisions. A comprehensive list of field of applications, ranging over, e.g., public administration, disaster recovery, allocation of huge sums of money, and military and political systems, can be found in [16], Section 9. Within computer security, we cite here some recent proposals exploiting this methodology. Work in [17] investigates the application of AHP to evaluate a so called multi factor reputation, to derive the priorities to attach to the scores assigned to different parameters affecting a global rating. Also, the authors of [18] address the issue of solving conflicts occurring in the authorization decision process among policies applicable to an access request. Operatively, the strategy for conflict resolution is implemented by exploiting AHP. Work in [19] is about prioritising role engineering , a discipline strictly related to Role-based Access Control models, and aimed to choose the best way to design a proper set of roles within structured organisations. Instead, the authors of [20] face the issue of measuring the effectiveness of security controls and metrics, and use AHP to select the most appropriate set of strategies leading to the effectiveness of a control.

6   Conclusions and Future Work

We have presented a multi-criteria evaluation of Android applications, on the basis of their meta-data, such as reputation indexes and declared permissions. We have proposed a novel definition for the threat score of an application, according to the application declared permissions. The proposed decision making procedure combines this threat score with information regarding the developer, the rating, and the number of downloads of the application. We have validated this procedure by testing it on well-known trusted and infected applications. The results confirm the good nature, or the malicious nature, of such applications. The proposed solution is based upon static analysis of XML files and, hence, it does not require the code to be decompiled and then analyzed.

We are currently investigating the possible combination of the decision framework with a *per-application monitoring intrusion detection systems* (IDS) [21]. Per-application IDSes generally monitor only a subset of all the applications running on a device, e.g. those that are considered suspicious. Since monitoring is a costly operation, from the point of view of resources, we aim to combine the proposed approach with an IDS, to monitor only the applications that received an *untrusted* classification.

References

1. Bugiel, S., Davi, L., Dmitrienko, A., Heuser, S., Sadeghi, A.R., Shastry, B.: Practical and Lightweight Domain Isolation on Android. In: 1st ACM Workshop on Security and Privacy in Smartphones and Mobile Devices (SPSM 2011), pp. 51–61. ACM (2011)
2. Zhou, Y., Zhang, X., Jiang, X., Freeh, V.W.: Taming Information-Stealing Smartphone Applications (on Android). In: McCune, J.M., Balacheff, B., Perrig, A., Sadeghi, A.-R., Sasse, A., Beres, Y. (eds.) Trust 2011. LNCS, vol. 6740, pp. 93–107. Springer, Heidelberg (2011)
3. Felt, A.P., Ha, E., Egelman, S., Haney, A., Chin, E., Wagner, D.: Android permissions: User attention, comprehension, and behavior. Technical report, Electrical Engineering and Computer SciencesUniversity of California at Berkeley (2012), `http://www.eecs.berkeley.edu/Pubs/TechRpts/2012/EECS-2012-26.html`
4. Felt, A.P., Chin, E., Hanna, S., Song, D., Wagner, D.: Android Permissions Demystified. In: 8th ACM Conference on Computer and Communications Security (CCS 2011), pp. 627–638. ACM (2011)
5. Jiang, X.: Multiple Security Alerts: New Android Malware Found in Official and Alternative Android Markets (2011), `http://www.csc.ncsu.edu/faculty/jiang/pubs/index.html`
6. Dini, G., Martinelli, F., Matteucci, I., Petrocchi, M., Saracino, A., Sgandurra, D.: A Multi-Criteria-Based Evaluation of Android Applications. Technical report, Istituto di Informatica e Telematica, CNR, Pisa (2012), `http://www.iit.cnr.it/node/17019`
7. Saaty, T.L.: Decision-making with the ahp: Why is the principal eigenvector necessary. European Journal of Operational Research 145(1), 85–91 (2003)
8. Saaty, T.L.: Decision making with the analytic hierarchy process. International Journal of Services Sciences 1(1) (2008)
9. Saaty, T.L.: How to make a decision: The analytic hierarchy process. European Journal of Operational Research 48(1), 9–26 (1990)
10. Saaty, T.L.: A scaling method for priorities in hierarchical structures. Journal of Mathematical Psychology 15(3), 234–281 (1977)
11. Felt, A.P., Finifter, M., Chin, E., Hanna, S., Wagner, D.: A survey of mobile malware in the wild. In: 1st ACM Workshop on Security and Privacy in Smartphones and Mobile Devices (SPSM 2011), pp. 3–14. ACM (2011)

12. Cannings, R.: An update on Android Market security (2011), `http://googlemobile.blogspot.com/2011/03/update-on-android-market-security.html`
13. Enck, W., Ongtang, M., McDaniel, P.: On Lightweight Mobile Phone Application Certification. In: 16th ACM Conference on Computer and Communications Security (CCS 2009), pp. 235–254. ACM (2009)
14. Nauman, M., Khan, S., Zhang, X.: Apex: Extending Android Permission Model and Enforcement with User-defined Runtime Constraints. In: 5th ACM Symposium on Information Computer and Communication Security (ASIACCS 2010), ACM (2010)
15. Barrera, D., Kayacik, H.G., van Oorschot, P.C., Somayaji, A.: A Methodology for Empirical Analysis of Permission-Based Security Models and its Application to Android. In: 17th ACM Conference on Computer and Communications Security (CCS 2010). ACM (2010)
16. Saaty, T.L.: Decision making with the analytic hierarchy process. International Journal of Services Sciences 1, 83–98 (2008)
17. Costantino, G., Martinelli, F., Petrocchi, M.: Priorities-based review computation. In: AAAI Spring Symposium, 2012 1st Workshop on Intelligent Web Services Meet Social Computing, vol. SS-12-04 (2012)
18. Matteucci, I., Mori, P., Petrocchi, M.: Prioritized execution of privacy policies. In: 2012 7th Intl. Workshop on Data Privacy Management, DPM (2012)
19. Colantonio, A.: Prioritizing role engineering objectives using the analytic hierarchy process. In: De Marco, M., Te'eni, D., Albano, V., Za, S. (eds.) Information Systems: Crossroads for Organization, Management, Accounting and Engineering, pp. 419–427. Physica-Verlag HD (2012)
20. Rajbhandari, L., Snekkenes, E.: An approach to measure effectiveness of control for risk analysis with game theory. In: 2011 1st Workshop on Socio-Technical Aspects in Security and Trust (STAST), pp. 24–29 (2011)
21. Dini, G., Martinelli, F., Saracino, A., Sgandurra, D.: MADAM: A Multi-Level Anomaly Detector for Android Malware. In: Kotenko, I., Skormin, V. (eds.) MMM-ACNS 2012. LNCS, vol. 7531, pp. 240–253. Springer, Heidelberg (2012)

Security Analysis of an Open Car Immobilizer Protocol Stack*

Stefan Tillich and Marcin Wójcik

University of Bristol, Computer Science Department, Merchant Venturers Building,
Woodland Road, BS8 1UB, Bristol, UK
{tillich,wojcik}@cs.bris.ac.uk

Abstract. An increasing number of embedded security applications—
which traditionally have been heavily reliant on secret and/or proprietary
solutions—apply the principle of open evaluation. A recent example is
the specification of an open security protocol stack for car immobilizer
applications by Atmel, which has been presented at ESCAR 2010. This
stack is primarily intended to be used in conjunction with automotive transponder chips of this manufacturer, but could in principle be
deployed on any suitable type of transponder chip. In this paper we
re-evaluate the security of this protocol stack. We were able to uncover
a number of security vulnerabilities. We show that an attacker with a
cheap standard reader close to such a car key can track it, lock sections of
its EEPROM, and even render its immobilizer functionality completely
useless. After eavesdropping on a genuine run of the authentication protocol between the car key and the car, an attacker is enabled to read and
write the memory of the car key. Furthermore, we point out the threats of
relay attacks and session hijacking, which require slightly more elaborate
attack setups. For each of the indicated attacks we propose possible fixes
and discuss their overhead.

Keywords: Security, car immobilizer, protocols, openness, analysis.

1 Introduction

Embedded security systems like car immobilizers have traditionally relied on
proprietary algorithms and protocols where the specifications have been kept
confidential. On the one hand, this approach can indeed complicate an attacker's
job for understanding the system's specifics. On the other hand, non-public
specifications limit the exposure of the employed security mechanisms to expert
scrutiny. Prominent attacks on such "closed" embedded security systems like on
the MIFARE Oyster card for London public transport [7] and the KeeLoq algorithm used in remote control systems [8] demonstrate the risks of this security
philosophy. In contrast, open evaluation efforts like the Advanced Encryption
Standard (AES) competition [12] and the Secure Hash Algorithm-3 (SHA-3)

---

* A previous version of this paper was presented at the industrial track of ACNS
  2012 [14].

C.J. Mitchell and A. Tomlinson (Eds.): INTRUST 2012, LNCS 7711, pp. 83–94, 2012.
© Springer-Verlag Berlin Heidelberg 2012

competition [13] are widely recognized for yielding robust solutions. Therefore, it is encouraging to see emerging open security specifications for embedded systems like the Open Source Immobilizer Protocol Stack given in [1]. Facilitated by its openness, we were able to re-evaluate its security, point out a number of security vulnerabilities, and suggest countermeasures.

A car immobilizer is a system that requires the presence of a security token (often in the form of a key fob) to allow a car to run. If this token is not present, the car's Engine Control Unit (ECU) interrupts key components like the ignition, the starter motor circuit, or the fuel pump. The communication between car and key fob is typically done via RFID, where the car is fitted with an RFID reader and the key fob contains an RFID tag. While earlier models used a static code in the key fob, modern immobilizers utilize either rolling codes or cryptography to prevent duplication of the key fob. Communication between car and key fob involves the use of a protocol stack which defines frame sizes, data formats, error detection, data transformations, etc.

Our analysis shows that an attacker can track car keys, lock sections of their EEPROM, and even permanently disrupt their immobilizer functionality with the help of a cheap standard reader and provided that she is in communication range. Eavesdropping on a genuine run of the authentication protocol between the key and the car allows an attacker to subsequently read and write memory of the key. In addition we discuss the issues of relay attacks and session hijacking.

The rest of the paper is organized as follows. The investigated protocol stack is described in Section 2. The attacks and security issues are we discovered are discussed in Section 3 and conclusions are drawn in Section 4.

2   Description of the Immobilizer Protocol Stack

An open security protocol stack for car immobilizer applications has been presented in [9]. It is mainly intended for use with specific automotive transponder chips. According to [9], the stack consists of a physical layer, a logical layer, a protocol layer, and the AES crypto layer. The physical layer deals with modulation types, data encoding, and bit timing. The logical layer defines the functional behavior of the reader and the transponder and includes communication link controls, controls configuration, setup of functional dependencies and error resolution. The protocol layer allocates data frames and buffers for reading and writing. It implements the user command interface, authentication, and key learning (*i.e.* changing cryptographic keys before and after deployment). The AES crypto layer controls the data authentication results[1]. Both physical and AES crypto layer are already industry standards. The logical and protocol layer, which are usually proprietary, are made open. This means the specification of these layers is available for inspection and modification.

---

[1] The description of this protocol layer in [9] probably refers to the use of the AES block cipher in the execution of various commands by reader and key fob. As such it is debatable whether it constitutes a separate layer or should be considered as part of the protocol layer.

The protocol stack implements a number of commands to be issued by the reader to the key fob. In most cases, the car featuring the immobilizer functionality acts as reader but the reader can also be a programming device used by the car manufacturer or distributor. The communication between reader and key fob uses the LF band at 125 kHz. In this band, the normal read range is usually very limited (commonly a few centimetres), but there are readers available which can extend it to up to one metre [3,6] and thus allowing for attacks in close proximity of the key fob.

The command set out in the protocol stack's specification [1] encompasses eleven commands. They include reading of the key fob's unique ID (UID) and error status, initiation of authentication, setting of the used secret keys, initiation and leaving of the so-called enhanced mode (for RF communication powered by the battery), a request to repeat the last response, reading and writing of user memory as well as setting memory access protection to certain memory sections. Authentication can be configured to be unilateral (only key fob authenticates itself to the reader) or "bilateral" (both key fob and reader authenticate themselves to each other) [2]. If "bilateral authentication" is configured, some commands like reading and writing user memory can only be executed when there has been a previous successful authentication.

Authentication follows the challenge-response pattern [11]. The party who wants to authenticate sends out a challenge (usually a random number) and the other participant transforms the challenge cryptographically using a secret or private key and returns the response. The first party then checks this result using its knowledge of the same secret key or the according public key. The point of the challenge is to prevent replay attacks, where messages recorded from a genuine protocol run are replayed by an attacker at a later time to achieve authentication. Therefore, the challenge must be non-repeating or only repeat with negligible probability.

The investigated protocol stack has the caveat that the key fob is not expected to be able to generate challenges. This is no problem for unilateral authentication, where the challenge is generated by the reader alone, but poses difficulties for "bilateral authentication". "Bilateral authentication" works by reusing the challenge from the reader for the challenge of the key fob. The cryptographic transformation involved in the authentication is AES encryption with one of two shared keys. Figure 1 shows the steps of "bilateral authentication" as given in [1].

The car and the key fob share two AES keys (Key 1 and Key 2). The "bilateral authentication" protocol works as follows. First, the car requests the key fob's unique ID (UID) via the "ReadUID" command. The key fob reads its UID from memory and returns it. The car checks whether this UID is paired with it (as a mechanism for early termination if a foreign key fob is in communication range).

---

[2] As we will show in the following, "bilateral authentication" as set out in [1] fails to achieve the goal of authenticating both parties which is central to protocols performing bilateral (mutual) authentication. We will thus use quotes to refer to this particular part of the protocol stack.

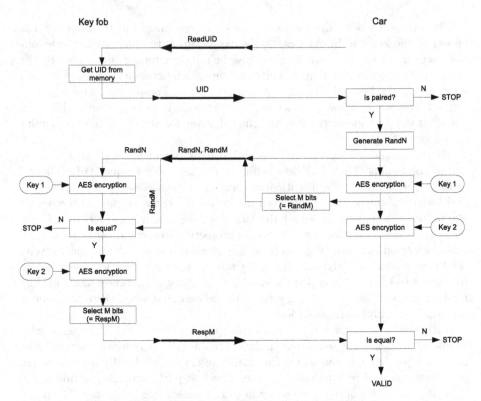

Fig. 1. "Bilateral authentication" between key fob and car

The second part of the protocol consists of a "Start Authentication" command by the car and the key fob's response. The car generates the N-bit challenge RandN, encrypts it with Key 1 and selects M bits of the resulting ciphertext as RandM. N and M can be configured to be less than the AES block size of 128 bits in order to reduce communication overhead. RandN and RandM are sent to the key fob, which validates that RandM originated from RandN via encryption with Key 1. If this is successful, the car is authenticated to the key fob. The key fob uses the output of the first AES encryption as input for a second AES encryption with Key 2. As this value is not fully known to an eavesdropper (M being usually smaller than 128), it is also denoted as hidden challenge. M bits of the second encryption result are selected as RespM, which is sent to the car. The car then verifies that RespM resulted from encryption with Key 2. On success, the key fob is authenticated to the car and "bilateral authentication" is finished.

3   Security Issues

The concrete attacks are listed in the rest of this section. All attacks require a standard reader in the vicinity of the genuine key fob. The relay attack in

Section 3.1 requires a second reader close to the car and connected to the first reader. The replay attack described in Section 3.4 also requires eavesdropping on a valid authentication or separate communication with the genuine key fob and the car prior to the actual attack. The session hijacking outlined in Section 3.6 requires the presence of the attacker's reader during communication of the genuine key fob and car. Also in this case the reader must be able to selectively overpower the signal from the car.

3.1   Relay Attack with Genuine Key Fob

Unlike the other attacks described in this paper, this attack is not specific to the investigated protocol stack but can potentially be applied to any security system with token-based authentication. A relay attack tricks the car into thinking that the key fob is in its immediate vicinity when it is actually located further away, thus allowing an attacker to deactivate the immobilizer. Such relay attacks have been known as early as 1976 [2] and have been practically demonstrated, e.g. in [5] for Automotive Passive Keyless Entry and Start Systems and in [4] for the EMV chip and PIN setting. In the current setting, this attack relays messages between the genuine key fob and the car through a transparent reader (close to the genuine key fob) connected to a transparent key fob (close to the car) as shown in Figure 2. Such an attack would require two cooperating attackers, one bringing the transparent reader close to the genuine key fob and the other gaining entry to the car and bringing the transparent key fob close to the car's reader.

Fig. 2. Relay attack with transparent reader and key fob

A potential countermeasure to this relay attack is to measure the communication delay between the reader's challenge and the key fob's response in order to detect the actual distance between the communicating endpoints. Alternatively, a dedicated protocol, like the distance bounding protocol used in [4] could be employed. However, the protocol stack includes a mechanism to defeat such countermeasures. If the transparent key fob fakes an uplink CRC error, this forces the car to send a "Repeat Last Response" command. The attacker can use the extra time for the repeated response to get the actual response from the genuine key fob.

This remote attack could be defended against with the measurement of the communication delay of the key fob by the car and by abandoning the mechanism of requesting a repeat of the the key fob's response in answer to a CRC error. Instead the whole sequence of commands and responses should be repeated when a CRC error is encountered. This gives the attacker no time to hide the extra communication delay introduced by the transparent reader and key fob.

Measurement of the communication delay might require extra components (e.g. a high-precision oscillator) at the car's side.

3.2 Tracking

Generally speaking, tracking is potentially enabled through any command which can be executed without proper authentication and which returns a result both predictable by the attacker and unique to the key fob. Although tracking can be achieved by a large range of technologies (e.g. automated visual license plate recognition), tracking via electronic tokens tends to be more versatile (e.g. requires no direct line of sight), more reliable (inherent error resilience of the employed digital communication protocols) and cheaper (wide availability of standardized readers). Traceability can be seen as an enabler of a large array of undesired behaviors (ranging from mere nuisances as revealing personal habits to potential untrustworthy companies up to more sinister threats as determining which individual in a crowd has recently come by an ATM machine).

The protocol stack includes the "ReadUID" command to retrieve the 32-bit UID from the key fob. There is no security mechanism in place which would require authentication by the reader. Therefore, any reader can request the UID and the key fob can be potentially tracked by an attacker via a number of standard readers installed at various places.

The specification [1] does not state whether tracking is considered an issue to protect against. A possible argument against the feasibility of tracking could be the potential small communication range of the key fob. However, we still think it is important to point out this issue in order to caution system developers against redeploying the protocol layer on a different physical layer without considering the potential ramifications of a change in communication range.

Tracking via the "ReadUID" command could be prevented if the UID is not returned in cleartext, but dependent on a shared secret and a nonce generated by the key fob. A simple example is to use the existing AES encryption E_K with one of the pre-shared keys K in a tweakable block cipher construction $\tilde{E}_K$ [10].

$$\tilde{E}_K(\text{nonce}, \text{UID}) = E_K(\text{nonce} \oplus E_K(\text{UID})) \tag{1}$$

The result of $\tilde{E}_K$ will vary with the nonce and the UID will be protected even when the nonce is revealed. Thus, even though the key fob can be still queried by any reader, the result cannot be used any more to track it.

There are two options for the values returned by the key fob depending on the actual functional requirements. If the complete result of $\tilde{E}_K$ is returned alongside with the nonce, the reader can decrypt it and arrive at the original UID. Thus, the full functionality of the original "ReadUID" command is retained. This comes at the price of a relatively high communication overhead as the key fob needs to send the 128-bit ciphertext $\tilde{E}_K$ and the nonce. The computational overhead would essentially be the generation of the nonce and two AES encryptions on the key fob side and two AES decryptions on the reader side.

Alternatively, the reader could still check for a specific UID if only a part of the result of $\tilde{E}_K$ were returned with the nonce. This could be useful if the reader requires the "ReadUID" command exclusively to check for a specific UID. We denote this new command as "CheckUID" and its functionality is shown in Figure 3. It's advantage is a shorter response and a better response time of the key fob compared to the enhanced "ReadUID" command.

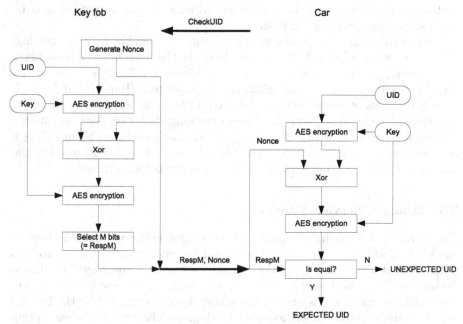

Fig. 3. Enhanced "CheckUID" command with resistance against tracking

By varying the size of the nonce and the portion of $\tilde{E}_K$ to be checked (M-bit RespM), the security and communication overhead can be balanced. For example, using a 32-bit portion of $\tilde{E}_K$ for checking, a similar resilience against accidentally matching UIDs would be introduced as in the original protocol stack with 32-bit UIDs. The communication overhead would consist of the extra bits of the nonce and the computational overhead would be the generation of the nonce for the key fob and two extra AES encryptions for key fob and reader each. The encrypted UID ($E_K(\mathrm{UID})$) could also be pre-computed and stored which would reduce the computational overhead by one AES encryption for each side.

In both cases, the key fob must be able to generate nonces. This might require a key fob with slightly higher capabilities as set out in the protocol stack specification. It might even be possible to include a software nonce generator (e.g. a LFSR with its state stored in non-volatile memory[3]). Note that generation of nonces is also required by the countermeasure to the attack described in Section 3.4. Considering the cost spent on implementation of a sound security

---

[3] The generator may need to be cryptographically strong.

primitive like AES, it appears logical to spend the extra effort for nonce generation in order to allow for sound protocols as well. It appears doubtful whether it is possible to defend against tracking without the ability of the key fob to generate nonces.

Other commands could also be used for tracking as well, although it would not be as versatile as using the "Read UID" command. To prevent tracking in such cases, the response of the key fob should either be randomized or only be given after authenticating the reader.

For example, the "Start Authentication" command could be used for tracking, as its response to a fixed challenge will always be the same but will most likely differ amongst different key fobs if they use different AES keys. However, an attacker needs to know a valid challenge-response pair (RandN and RandM, cf. Figure 1), as otherwise the key fob would abort the authentication before providing a trackable response. To prevent tracking via "Start Authentication", the key fob could randomize its response to the car's challenge by including a self-generated random part to it. This would still allow for authentication by the car (provided the new random part of the challenge is also returned)[4].

3.3   Denial-of-Service Attacks

The protocol stack includes commands for writing new cryptographic keys to the key fob, which replaces the old keys used for authentication. There are two different modes for doing this: In open mode, a "Learn Secret Key1" or "Learn Secret Key2" can be issued by any reader in order to set new keys. In secure mode, an encrypted key is sent by the reader device, decrypted by the key fob and the result is set as new key as shown in Figure 4. The key used for encrypting the new key is the so-called Default Secret Key which is factory set.

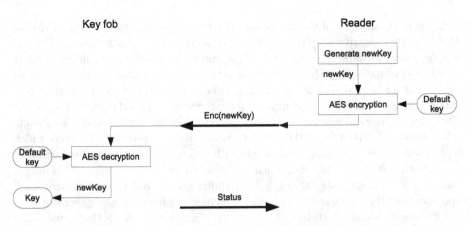

Fig. 4. LearnSecretKey command in secure mode

---

[4] In the case of "Start Authentication", tracking could also be prevented by the adoption of the countermeasure against replay attacks in Section 3.4.

Overwriting keys in open mode is trivial, as the malicious reader only has to send the according command to set the keys to those of her choice. However, even in secure mode it is possible to overwrite keys though the value of the new keys stays hidden to the attacker. This is possible without knowledge of the Default Secret Key because the secure key learn command only uses the encrypted key but no integrity check for it. Therefore, an attacker can send a random value as encrypted key and the key fob will set the decrypted value as new key.

Thus, in both open and secure mode, keys can be overwritten without the need of knowing a shared secret. Once this has been done, the key fob will no longer work with the car. If the key fob is queried in intervals while the car is in motion, it might even be possible to force the immobilizer to stop the car by overwriting the keys.

The open mode is vulnerable against this attack per design. To defend against the attack in secure mode, a message authentication code (MAC) should be included with the encrypted key and the key should only be overwritten when the MAC is verified successfully. This entails communication overhead for trans-mission of the MAC from the reader to the key fob and computational overhead of MAC generation in the reader and MAC verification in the key fob.

3.4   Replay Attack on Authentication

A unique property of the "bilateral authentication" protocol in the immobilizer stack is that the key fob is not required to generate nonces. Instead, the encrypted nonce from the reader is "reused" as the challenge from the key fob. While this makes the structure of the key fob simpler, it also means the commands from the reader can be recorded and replayed at a later time to achieve authentication. Thus, the "bilateral authentication" protocol does not provide mutual entity authentication but only entity authentication of the reader to the key fob and data origin authentication of the key fob's response to the car.

In order to be able to record the appropriate reader command, the attacker can record it during a run of authentication between the genuine key fob and the car. Alternatively, the car can be prompted to issue a valid authentication challenge without the presence of the genuine key fob, if the attacker is able to send the correct UID. For example, the attacker could query the UID from the genuine key fob via the "Read UID" command (similar as in the tracking scenario in Section 3.2). Thus an attacker can pretend to be an authenticated reader, which gives her access to advanced commands like "Read User Memory" and "Write User Memory". Note that the specification [1] does not mention the scenario of replay attacks, so it remains unclear whether the protocol designers consider protection against it as out of scope of "bilateral authentication".

A defense against this attack is to have the key fob generate the challenges for the reader. Without a challenge from the key fob, the replay of the reader command will lead to a successful authentication of the reader.

3.5 Spoofing Attack on Memory Access Protection

The protocol stack allows the reader to lock the EEPROM sections AP1 to AP3 via a "Write Memory Access Protection" command. This command is accepted by the key fob without prior authentication and could be issued by any attacker with a standard reader close to it. Depending on the actual use of these EEPROM sections, an attacker could impair the functionality of the key fob by locking them with a spoofed command.

By requiring prior authentication for the "Write Memory Access Protection" command this attack can be prevented.

3.6 Hijacking Communication Sessions

Privileged commands (e.g. "Write User Memory") can only be executed if there has been a successful authentication previously (using the "Start Authentication" command). However, if a malicious reader is present during the communication session between car and key fob, it could be possible for it to remain dormant until after the successful authentication and then to "hijack" the session by overshadowing the car's communication with its own. In that way an attacker could gain access to privileged commands similar as in the replay attack described in Section 3.4. In particular, session hijacking could still occur even if the protocol was secured against the replay attack.

A possible way to prevent session hijacking would be to enhance the authentication to an authenticated key agreement, in which a session key is generated. This session key would then be used to authenticated subsequent commands (and possibly also responses), e.g. by including a MAC over each message. An attacker without knowledge of the session key would then be unable to take over the session and could only disrupt it by jamming the communication channel. Note that such a non-persistent denial-of-service-attack[5] is a general threat which cannot be solved solely on the logical protocol layers but would have to be addressed at the physical layer.

4 Conclusions

In this paper we have identified a number of potential security vulnerabilities in an open car immobilizer stack. The vulnerabilities include tracking of key fobs, denial-of-service attacks to render key fobs useless, achieving key fob authentication despite absence of the key fob (relay attack), achieving reader authentication via a replay attack, and a spoof attack to lock out EEPROM sections of the key fob. For each of the identified vulnerabilities we propose countermeasures. This proves the great value of the openness of the protocol stack to public review.

---

[5] We denote jamming of the communication channel as a non-persistent attack as it requires the presence of a disruptive device and will disappear as soon as said device is no longer close to the authentic communication parties.

Some of our proposed countermeasures can be implemented rather easily while others require enhanced functionalities from the reader and/or the key fob.

Future work involves implementation of the attacks with the help of a prototyping system and formal verification of the proposed countermeasures to ensure their correctness.

Acknowledgements. The authors would like to acknowledge the help of Loïc Duflot, Shujun Li and the anonymous reviewers, whose comments helped to improve this paper.

The research described in this paper has been supported by EPSRC grant EP/H001689/1. The information in this document reflects only the author's views, is provided as is, and no guarantee or warranty is given that the information is fit for any particular purpose. The user thereof uses the information at its sole risk and liability.

References

1. Atmel. Open Source Immobilizer Protocol Stack (2010),
   http://www.atmel.com/ dyn/products/tools_card.asp?tool_id=17197
   (registration required)
2. Conway, J.H.: On Numbers and Games. Academic Press (1976)
3. Daily RFID Co., limited. LF RFID Reader-03,
   http://www.rfid-in-china.com/2008-09-06/products_detail_2140.html
4. Drimer, S., Murdoch, S.J.: Keep Your Enemies Close: Distance Bounding Against Smartcard Relay Attacks. In: Proceedings of the 16th USENIX Security Symposium, pp. 87–102 (2007)
5. Francillon, A., Danev, B., Capkun, S.: Relay Attacks on Passive Keyless Entry and Start Systems in Modern Cars. In: Proceedings of the 18th Annual Network & Distributed System Security Symposium (NDSS 2011), ISOC (2011)
6. GAO RFID Inc. 125 kHz Long Range Reader,
   http://www.gaorfid.com/index.php?main_page=product_info&products_id=363
7. Garcia, F.D., de Koning Gans, G., Muijrers, R., van Rossum, P., Verdult, R., Schreur, R.W., Jacobs, B.: Dismantling MIFARE Classic. In: Jajodia, S., Lopez, J. (eds.) ESORICS 2008. LNCS, vol. 5283, pp. 97–114. Springer, Heidelberg (2008)
8. Indesteege, S., Keller, N., Dunkelman, O., Biham, E., Preneel, B.: A Practical Attack on KeeLoq. In: Smart, N.P. (ed.) EUROCRYPT 2008. LNCS, vol. 4965, pp. 1–18. Springer, Heidelberg (2008)
9. Lepek, P.: Configurable, Secure, Open Immobilizer Implementation. In: Proceedings of the 8th Embedded Security in Cars (ESCAR) Conference
10. Liskov, M., Rivest, R.L., Wagner, D.: Tweakable Block Ciphers. In: Yung, M. (ed.) CRYPTO 2002. LNCS, vol. 2442, pp. 31–46. Springer, Heidelberg (2002)
11. Menezes, A.J., van Oorschot, P.C., Vanstone, S.A.: Handbook of Applied Cryptography. Series on Discrete Mathematics and its Applications. CRC Press (1997) ISBN 0-8493-8523-7, http://www.cacr.math.uwaterloo.ca/hac/

12. National Institute of Standards and Technology. AES Competition Website (archived), http://csrc.nist.gov/archive/aes/index.html
13. National Institute of Standards and Technology. SHA-3 Competition Website, http://csrc.nist.gov/groups/ST/hash/sha-3/index.html
14. Tillich, S., Wójcik, M.: Security Analysis of an Open Car Immobilizer Protocol Stack. Presented at the Industry Track of the 10th International Conference on Applied Cryptograpy and Network Security (ACNS 2012) (June 2012)

A Static Diffie-Hellman Attack on Several Direct Anonymous Attestation Schemes

Ernie Brickell[1], Liqun Chen[2], and Jiangtao Li[1]

[1] Intel Corporation, Hillsboro, Oregon, USA
{ernie.brickell,jiangtao.li}@intel.com
[2] Hewlett-Packard Laboratories, Bristol, UK
liqun.chen@hp.com

Abstract. Direct Anonymous Attestation (DAA) is an anonymous signature scheme designed for anonymous attestation of a Trusted Platform Module (TPM) while preserving the privacy of the device owner. In 2004, Brickell, Camenisch, and Chen provided the first DAA scheme based on the strong RSA assumption and decisional Diffie-Hellman assumption. This scheme was adopted by the Trusted Computing Group in the TPM 1.2 Specification and has been implemented in hundreds of millions of computer platforms. Since then, multiple DAA schemes have been developed, many of which are based on bilinear maps. In this paper, we discover that in a large number of DAA schemes, including the original one adopted in TPM 1.2, a malicious user can treat a TPM as a static Diffie-Hellman (DH) oracle, therefore security of these schemes are based on the hardness of the static DH problem. However, this security feature has not been analyzed in the security proofs of most of these schemes. Brown and Gallant showed that one can break the Static DH problem in a group of order ρ with only $O(\rho^{1/3})$ oracle queries and $O(\rho^{1/3})$ group operations. Our discovery means that the security level of these DAA schemes can be significantly weaken, only roughly 2/3 of the claimed security level. We discuss the impact of our discovery and present how to patch the affected DAA schemes to avoid this attack.

1 Introduction

Direct anonymous attestation (DAA) is a special digital signature primitive, providing a balance between user privacy and signer authentication in a reasonable way. In a DAA scheme, there are issuers, signers and verifiers. The role of an issuer is to verify legitimation of signers and to issue a unique DAA credential to each legitimate signer. A signer proves possession of her credential to a verifier by providing a DAA signature without revealing her identity.

The concept and first concrete scheme of DAA were presented by Brickell, Camenisch, and Chen [6] for the purposes of remote anonymous attestation of a trusted computing platform. In this paper, we call this scheme RSA-DAA for short. The RSA-DAA scheme was adopted by the Trusted Computing Group (TCG) and specified in the Trusted Platform Module (TPM) specification

C.J. Mitchell and A. Tomlinson (Eds.): INTRUST 2012, LNCS 7711, pp. 95–111, 2012.
© Springer-Verlag Berlin Heidelberg 2012

version 1.2 [30]. This specification has recently been adopted by ISO/IEC as an international standard [1]. Since the first introduction of DAA, it has attracted lots of attention from both industry and cryptographic researchers, e.g., [2, 7–12, 17–22, 26].

Unlike group signatures such as defined in [4], DAA does not have the "open" feature in which the identity of its signer can be recovered from the signature by an authorized entity, such as a group manager. Signatures created by a DAA signer are anonymous even if a verifier and an issuer collude. Instead, DAA has a feature called user-controlled-traceability, where a DAA signer and a verifier can jointly decide whether the verifier is allowed to link two signatures produced by this signer. Many DAA schemes use the following mechanism for user-controlled-traceability: Let f be a unique secret key of the signer. A DAA signature contains $(\zeta, N_V) \in \mathbb{G}^2$, where $\mathbb{G}$ is a cyclic group of order ρ and $N_V = \zeta^f$. The value ζ is called the base and N_V is called the pseudonym. If the signer and verifier agree on a fixed base ζ, then all the DAA signatures from the signer are linkable, because they all contain the same pseudonym N_V. If the signer wants her signatures unlinkable, she chooses a random base ζ for each signature.

In DAA, the role of a signer is split between two parties, a principal signer with limited resource such as a trusted platform module (TPM), and an assistant signer with abundant computational power but less security tolerance such as a computer platform. We call the assistant signer the Host in our paper. As the resource of TPM are very limited, many DAA schemes are designed to minimize the requirement on the TPM resources. In the original DAA scheme [6], ζ is chosen by the Host and sent to the TPM. The TPM only verifies that $\zeta \in \mathbb{G}$, and later computes $N_V = \zeta^f$ and outputs it to the Host. Several other DAA schemes, e.g. [7, 17, 21], follow such design.

Given a cyclic group $\mathbb{G}$ of order ρ, the static DH oracle on $x \in \mathbb{Z}_\rho^*$ is defined as a function that takes any $r \in \mathbb{G}$ as input and outputs r^x. The static DH problem is to compute the discrete log x, given $g, h \in \mathbb{G}$ such that $h = g^x$ and given access to the static DH oracle on x. In 2004, Brown and Gallant [13] showed an algorithm that breaks the static DH problem in a group of order ρ with only u oracle queries and $2(\sqrt{u} + \sqrt{v})$ group operations, where $\rho = uv + 1$. This algorithm is more efficient than the generic baby-step-giant-step algorithm [28] that solves the discrete log problem. For example, the generic algorithm that solves the discrete log problem takes $O(\rho^{1/2})$ operations. The Brown-Gallant algorithm can solve the static DH problem in $O(\rho^{1/3})$ operations, if there exist u, v such that u is close to $\rho^{1/3}$ and v is close to $\rho^{2/3}$.

In this paper, we discover that the TPM in the DAA schemes [6–9, 17, 18, 20, 21] behaves as a static DH oracle, i.e., given any $\zeta \in \mathbb{G}$, the TPM outputs ζ^f. If the Host is corrupted, attacker can launch the Brown-Gallant algorithm to extract the DAA secret key. Interestingly, most of the security proofs of these DAA schemes do not rely on this static DH assumption. We believe that there must be errors in the security proofs. In the parameters of the RSA-DAA scheme specified in TPM 1.2, ρ is 208-bit. It is generally believed that the RSA-DAA scheme [6] has 104-bit security strength. With our discovery, the DAA scheme in

TPM 1.2 only offers around 70-bit of security in the worst case. Our contributions of the paper are summarized as follows.

DISCOVERY OF THE STATIC DH ASSUMPTION USED IN MULTIPLE DAA SCHEMES: We discover that the static DH assumption was used by multiple DAA schemes [6, 7, 17, 21] without being explicitly specified in the security proofs. Our discovery means that the security level of these DAA schemes could be significantly weaken. We present where these proofs go wrong.

PRACTICAL IMPACT OF OUR DISCOVERY AND POSSIBLE MITIGATION: We study the practical impact of our discovery and provide a couple of mitigation methods. For the DAA scheme that has already been deployed, we can choose ρ as a safe prime to mitigate the Brown-Gallant attack. We also suggest a modification to these DAA schemes to remove the dependency on the static DH assumption. Note that the static DH problem is still believed to be a computationally hard problem. Our paper doesn't provide a practical attack to any affected DAA schemes but provides theoretical contribution to this research field.

The rest of this paper is organized as follows. We first review the static DH assumption and review the corresponding attack by Brown and Gallant in Section 2. In Section 3, we present where the static DH assumption was used in the original RSA-DAA scheme [6], where the corresponding security proof went wrong, and how the Brown-Gallant attack can be used to weak the security of this DAA scheme. We then present where the static DH assumption was used in various other DAA schemes in Section 4. We discuss the impacts of our discovery in Section 5 and present how to modify the DAA schemes to avoid this attack in Section 6. We conclude the paper in Section 7. Finally we recall the original RSA-DAA scheme [6] in Appendix A.

2   Background on the Static DH Problem

In this section, we first describe the static Diffie-Hellman (DH) Problem and then review the Brown-Gallant attack to the problem.

Definition 1 (Static DH Oracle). *Let $\mathbb{G}$ be a cyclic group of prime order ρ. Let x be a value in $\mathbb{Z}_\rho^*$. Given any $r \in \mathbb{G}$, the static DH oracle on x computes and outputs r^x.*

Definition 2 (Static DH Problem). *Let $\mathbb{G}$ be a cyclic group of prime order ρ. Given $g, h \in \mathbb{G}$ such that $h = g^x$, the static DH problem is to compute x given access to a static DH oracle on x.*

The static DH assumption is that it is computationally infeasible to solve the static DH problem. The static DH assumption is a stronger assumption than the discrete log assumption, because if one can solve the discrete log problem, then he can solve the static DH problem as well. It is still believed in the cryptography community that the static DH problem is a computationally hard problem, although this static DH assumption is not widely used. Several cryptographic protocols rely on this static DH assumption, such as the basic El Gamal encryption [24], Ford-Kaliski server-assisted key generation protocol [25], and Chaum and van Antwerpen's Undeniable Signatures [16]. These protocols provide a static DH oracle on the secret key to the adversary as a part of their operation. In the next two sections, we shall describe how the static DH assumption is related to several DAA schemes [6–9, 17, 18, 20, 21].

The static DH problem has been studied by Brown and Gallant in [13]. This paper provides an algorithm that solves the static DH problem more efficient than the generic Shanks' baby-step-giant-step algorithm [28]. The Brown-Gallant algorithm [13] is stated in the following theorem.

Theorem 1. *Let $\mathbb{G}$ be a cyclic group of prime order ρ such that $\rho = uv + 1$ for positive integers u and v. There exists an algorithm that solve the static DH problem on $\mathbb{G}$ with u queries to the static DH oracle and about $2(\sqrt{u} + \sqrt{v})$ off-line group operations in $\mathbb{G}$.*

Proof. This theorem and proof are provided by Brown and Gallant [13]. Given $g, h \in \mathbb{G}$ such that $h = g^x$ and $x \in \mathbb{Z}_\rho^*$, the following algorithm is to compute x by querying the static DH oracle on x. Let s be a generator of the multiplicative group $\mathbb{F}_\rho^*$, we have $x = s^z \pmod{\rho}$ for some integer $z \in [0, \rho - 2]$. Let $z = tv + y$ for some $t \in [0, u-1]$ and $y \in [0, v-1]$. The strategy is to first compute y and t, and then compute z. Once z is computed, x can be easily computed.

To compute $y = z \bmod v$, first apply u queries to the static DH oracle on x interactively and obtain $g^x, g^{x^2}, g^{x^3}, \ldots, g^{x^u}$. Observe that

$$x^u = (s^z)^u = s^{zu} = s^{(tv+y)u} = s^{tuv+yu} = s^{yu} = (s^u)^y.$$

It is easy to see that x^u lies on $\langle s^u \rangle$, the order v subgroup of $\mathbb{F}_\rho^*$. Let $E = g^{x^u} = g^{(s^u)^y}$, we can apply the Shanks' baby-step-giant-step algorithm [28] to compute y with $2\sqrt{v}$ group operations: Let $m = \lceil \sqrt{v} \rceil$, y can be represented as $y = jm + i$ where $0 \le i, j < m$. We can compute i and j as follows. We first compute

$$g, g^{s^u}, g^{(s^u)^2}, \ldots, g^{(s^u)^{m-1}}.$$

We then compute

$$E, E^{(s^u)^{-m}}, E^{(s^u)^{-2m}}, \ldots, E^{(s^u)^{-(m-1)m}}.$$

The second list is equal to

$$g^{(s^u)^y}, g^{(s^u)^{y-m}}, g^{(s^u)^{y-2m}}, \ldots, g^{(s^u)^{y-(m-1)m}}.$$

There must be a match in the above two lists. In other words, we can find i, j such that $g^{(s^u)^i} = g^{(s^u)^{y-jm}}$. Now we have $y = i + jm \bmod v$.

Next we compute t. First compute $F = h^{s^{-y}}$. Observe that

$$F = h^{s^{-y}} = (g^x)^{s^{-y}} = (g^{s^z})^{s^{-y}} = g^{s^z \cdot s^{-y}} = g^{s^{tv+y} \cdot s^{-y}} = g^{s^{tv}} = g^{(s^v)^t}.$$

We can see that $(s^v)^t$ lies on $\langle s^v \rangle$, the order u subgroup of $\mathbb{F}_p^*$. We can apply the baby-step-giant-step algorithm again to compute t using F with $2\sqrt{u}$ group operations. This is the same way that we compute y above. Once y and t are computed, we have $z = tv + y$. We can compute $x = s^z \pmod{\rho}$. This algorithm takes u queries to the static DH oracle and $2(\sqrt{u} + \sqrt{v})$ group operations in $\mathbb{G}$.

If there exists $u \approx \rho^{1/3}$, then an adversary can solve static DH problem in about $\rho^{1/3}$ group operations. A normal attack to the discrete log problem would require $\rho^{1/2}$ group operations. Using 256-bit ρ as an example, one can query the static DH oracle $O(2^{85})$ times and solve the discrete log problem with $O(2^{85})$ computations instead of $O(2^{128})$ computations.

3   Static DH Assumption on the RSA-DAA Scheme

In this section, we demonstrate that the original DAA scheme (called RSA-DAA for short), which was proposed in [6] and adopted by TCG for TPM version 1.2 [1, 30], includes "a static DH oracle". By saying this we mean that a TPM 1.2 chip can be used by a malicious user as a static DH oracle, and therefore, if the static DH problem is solvable, then an adversary can retrieve the corresponding DAA private key from the TPM. We now first briefly review the RSA-DAA scheme, and then discuss how it is connected to the static DH assumption.

3.1   Brief Review of RSA-DAA

In this subsection, we only review the basic idea of the RSA-DAA scheme in this subsection for the purpose of demonstrating that there is a static DH oracle in it. Readers are suggested to get details of the scheme in [6] (for convenience, a reasonable detailed recall is given in Appendix A).

In the TPM 1.2 implementation of RSA-DAA, there are two protocols: one is called DAA-Join and the other is DAA-Sign. In DAA-Join, a TPM generates a DAA private key denoted by f and obtains a Camenisch-Lysyanskaya (CL) signature [14] on it from a DAA issuer. The value f is split into two ℓ_f-bit (104-bit) messages denoted by f_0 and f_1, and this signature is used as a DAA credential. In DAA-Sign, a TPM anonymously convinces a verifier that it got such a credential. In both the protocols, a TPM must also provide a pseudonym, denoted by N_I in DAA-Join and N_V in DAA-Sign, and a proof that the pseudonym is formed correctly, i.e., that it is derived from the TPM's private key f and a base determined by the issuer in DAA-Join or by the verifier in DAA-Sign. We shall discuss in the next subsection that this pseudonym actually provides a static DH oracle.

The DAA-Join protocol between the TPM and issuer (as shown in Figure 1 of Appendix A) is as follows. The issuer's public key includes the values of R_0, R_1, S, n, Z, ρ and Γ, where ρ (208-bit) is a prime order of the subgroup of $\mathbb{Z}_\Gamma^*$. First, the TPM sends the issuer a commitment to the message-pair (f_0, f_1), i.e., $U := R_0^{f_0} R_1^{f_1} S^{v'} \bmod n$, where v' is a value chosen randomly by the TPM to "blind" the f_i's and n is a RSA modulus. Also, the TPM computes $N_I := \zeta_I^f \mod \Gamma$, where ζ_I is a quantity derived from the issuer's name and $f = f_0 + f_1 2^{\ell_f}$. This computation process involves the step that the host platform computes $\zeta_I := (H_\Gamma(1\|\mathrm{bsn}_I))^{(\Gamma-1)/\rho} \mod \Gamma$, where H_Γ is a hash-function mapping an arbitrary length string into $\mathbb{Z}_\Gamma$, and sends ζ_I to the TPM. The value N_I allows the issuer to detect a rogue TPM (i.e. its DAA private key is compromised and publicly available) and controls how many DAA keys for one TPM could be created. The TPM then sends U and N_I to the issuer. Next, the TPM convinces the issuer that U and N_I are correctly formed (using a proof of knowledge of a representation of U w.r.t. the bases R_0, R_1, S and N_I w.r.t. ζ_I) and that the f_i's lie in $\pm\{0,1\}^{\ell_f+\ell_H+\ell_\varnothing+2}$, where ℓ_f, ℓ_H, and $\ell_\varnothing$ are security parameters.

To issue a credential, the issuer chooses a random integer v'' and a random prime e, signs the hidden messages by computing $A := \left(\frac{Z}{U S^{v''}}\right)^{1/e} \mod n$, and sends the TPM (A, e, v''). The issuer also proves to the TPM that she computed A correctly. The signature on (f_0, f_1) is then $(A, e, v := v' + v'')$, where v should be kept secret by the TPM (for f_0 and f_1 to remain hidden from the issuer), while A and e can be public.

The DAA-Sign protocol between the TPM and verifier (as shown in Figure 2 of Appendix A) is as follows. A TPM proves that it got a signature from the issuer on some values f_0 and f_1 without revealing either the signature or the signed values. This can be done by a zero-knowledge proof of knowledge of values f_0, f_1, A, e, and v such that $A^e R_0^{f_0} R_1^{f_1} S^v \equiv Z \pmod{n}$. Also, the TPM computes $N_V := \zeta^{f_0 + f_1 2^{\ell_f}} \mod \Gamma$ and proves that the value N_V is correctly formed and the values of f_0 and f_1 in N_V are the same as them in (A, e, v). This computation process involves the step that the host platform computes $\zeta := (H_\Gamma(1\|\mathrm{bsn}_V))^{(\Gamma-1)/\rho} \mod \Gamma$, and sends ζ to the TPM. The value N_V is used for the rogue TPM detection, and as well as for user-controlled-traceability. The detailed definition of user-controlled-traceability is given in [8].

3.2   Static DH Oracle Involved in RSA-DAA

We now present how the static DH oracle is involved in the RSA-DAA scheme. It is required that $\zeta_I, \zeta \in \langle\gamma\rangle$, i.e., the subgroup of $\mathbb{Z}_\Gamma^*$ of order ρ. As discussed in Section 2, whether computation of the values of ρ, Γ, ζ_I (or ζ) and N_I (or N_V) is a static DH oracle is dependent on how the value of ζ_I (or ζ) and the value ρ are created. Although it was mentioned in [6] that the ζ value is either chosen randomly by the TPM or input to the TPM by the host platform, in the implementation of TPM 1.2, this value is actually computed by the host platform and the TPM only checks whether the input is in a right group by verifying $\zeta^\rho \equiv 1 \mod \Gamma$. The same as ζ_I. The value of ρ is part of the issuer's public key, so it is assumed that this value is chosen by the issuer. Now we can see the worst case that the issuer is malicious and that the issuer and the host platform are colluded. In this case, an adversary plays the roles of a malicious issuer and host, the adversary can deliberately choose the value ρ satisfying $\rho = uv + 1$, where $u \approx \rho^{1/3}$, and then mount the static DH attack by using a TPM as a static DH oracle and following the Brown-Gallant algorithm described in Section 2. Even if the issuer is not malicious and chooses a random ρ, an attacker can factorize $\rho - 1$ and apply the Brown-Gallant algorithm.

This observation tells us that security of the RSA-DAA scheme is dependent on the hardness of the static DH problem. That is, if one finds an efficient algorithm that solves the static DH problem, she can use this algorithm to extract the DAA private key from the TPM by using the TPM as a static DH oracle, thus breaks the DAA scheme. In [6], security of the RSA-DAA scheme is proved under the strong RSA assumption and decisional DH (DDH) assumption without mentioning the static DH assumption. More specifically, in the security proof, the simulator uses a random value to simulate N_I or N_V. It was argued that no adversary can distinguish the distribution of random N_I or N_V with distribution of N_I or N_V in the real system under the DDH assumption. However, as we demonstrated before, instead of generating ζ_I or ζ by following the protocols and making them be the random distribution, the adversary can generate them by following the Brown-Gallant algorithm and then use a TPM as a static DH oracle.

Note that if the adversary does not compute ζ_I as $\zeta_I := (H_\Gamma(1\|\mathbf{bsn}_I))^{(\Gamma-1)/\rho}$ mod Γ, or ζ as $\zeta := (H_\Gamma(1\|\mathbf{bsn}_V))^{(\Gamma-1)/\rho}$ mod Γ, but following the Brown-Gallant algorithm to choose them with specific values, a TPM will not be able to tell the difference. The incorrectly generated ζ value will be rejected by a honest verifier if it is used in a DAA signature, but in the static DH attack that we are concerned in this paper, there is no any verifier's involvement. After letting the TPM accepts these incorrect ζ_I or ζ values, the adversary may benefit from the static DH attack. We believe that this type of malicious behavior and connection between the RSA-DAA scheme and the static DH assumption is not captured in the security proof. Therefore, the original security proof of RSA-DAA was incomplete.

4   Static DH Assumption on ECC-DAA Schemes

Since the original DAA scheme [6] was adopted by the Trusted Computing Group in 2003 [30], researchers have developed a large number of DAA schemes, such as [7, 9, 12, 17–22], to list a few. Most of them are based on computational hard problems with elliptic curves rather than the RSA problem. In this section, we demonstrate that several elliptic curve based DAA schemes (called ECC-DAA for short) also include "a static DH oracle". In the following two subsections, we first briefly review the ECC-DAA schemes, and then discuss how they are connected to the static DH assumption.

4.1   Brief Review of ECC-DAA

Generally speaking, all the ECC-DAA schemes that we know make use of a computable bilinear map function, denoted by $e : \mathbb{G}_1 \times \mathbb{G}_2 \to \mathbb{G}_T$, where $\mathbb{G}_1, \mathbb{G}_2$ and $\mathbb{G}_T$ are three groups each with a large prime order p. Some of them use a symmetric pairing, i.e. $\mathbb{G}_1 = \mathbb{G}_2$. For simplicity, we do not distinguish between these schemes using symmetric or asymmetric pairings. Security of these ECC-DAA schemes are based on either the LRSW assumption [27] or the the Strong Diffie-Hellman (SDH) assumption [23]. Again due to the limited space, our review includes only the necessary information, which enables us to discuss on how the static DH oracle is involved in these schemes in the next subsection, and we refer the details of these schemes to their original papers.

In an ECC-DAA scheme based on the LRSW assumption, such as [7, 9, 18–21], the issuer's private key is $(x, y) \in \mathbb{Z}_p$ for a prime p and the public key includes $(p, P_1, P_2, X = [x]P_2, Y = [y]P_2)$, where $P_1 \in \mathbb{G}_1$ and $P_2, X, Y \in \mathbb{G}_2$. In the DAA-Join protocol, a TPM creates its DAA private key, say $f \in \mathbb{Z}_p$, commits the value f with $F = [f]P_1$ and proves to the issuer that the value F was correctly computed. The corresponding DAA credential is (A, B, C), which is a Camenisch-Lysyanskaya signature [15] of the value f such that

$$A = [r]P_1, B = [y]A, C = [x + xyf]A \text{ for a random } r \in \mathbb{Z}_p.$$

A DAA signature is a proof of knowledge of values f, A, B and C, along with

$$K = [f]J,$$

where J is an element of $\mathbb{G}_1$, $\mathbb{G}_T$ or a different cyclic group, computed from a given base name bsn via a hash-function.

In an ECC-DAA scheme based on the SDH assumption, such as [11, 12, 17, 22], the issuer's private key is $\gamma \in \mathbb{Z}_p$ and its public key includes $(p, g_1, h_1, h_2, g_2, w = [\gamma]g_2)$, where $g_1, h_1, h_2 \in \mathbb{G}_1$, and $g_2, w \in \mathbb{G}_2$. In the DAA-Join protocol, a TPM creates its DAA private key, again say $f \in \mathbb{Z}_p$, commits the value f with $F = [f]h_1$ and proves to the issuer that the value F was correctly computed. The corresponding DAA credential is (A, x) where x is randomly chosen from $\mathbb{Z}_p$ and $A = [1/(\gamma + x)](g_1 + [f]h_1)$; note that (A, x) is a BBS signature [5] on the value f. A DAA signature is a proof of knowledge of the values f, A, and x such that

$$A = [1/(\gamma + x)](g_1 + [f]h_1) \text{ and } K = [f]J,$$

where J is an element of $\mathbb{G}_1$ or a different cyclic group, computed from a give base name bsn via a hash-function.

4.2   Static DH Oracle Involved in ECC-DAA

We now present how the static DH oracle is involved in these ECC-DAA schemes [7–9, 17, 18, 20, 21]. By following the terminology used in the TPM 1.2 implementation, a DAA scheme includes a DAA-Join protocol and a DAA-Sign protocol. Compared with the RSA-DAA scheme, the ECC-DAA schemes do not usually include the value N_I in the DAA-Join protocol, that is because a TPM commits the DAA private key f on a fixed base, i.e., $F = [f]P_1$ in the LRSW based schemes and $F = [f]h_1$ in the SDH based schemes. This tells that the DAA-Join protocol in these ECC-DAA schemes does not involve a static DH oracle.

However, in the DAA-Sign protocol, both the LRSW based schemes and the SDH based schemes include a pair of (J, K) values, where $K = [f]J$ and J is an element of $\mathbb{G}_1$, G_T or a different cyclic group. For simplicity, we take G_1 as an example and recall this group has a prime order p. The pair (J, K) play the same role of the pair (ζ, N_V) in the RSA-DAA scheme, i.e., for the rogue TPM detection, and as well as for user-controlled-traceability.

As discussed in Section 2, whether computation of the values of p, $\mathbb{G}_1$, J and K is a static DH oracle is dependent on how the value of J and the value of p are created. Although a few papers, such as [12, 22], suggested that the value J should be either chosen randomly by the TPM or computed by the TPM from a given base name, in the most of the ECC-DAA schemes, it is either explicitly or implicitly suggested that this value is computed by the host platform and the TPM only checks whether the input is in a right group or not; for some special group implementation this feature is guaranteed so such a check is actually omitted. The value of p is part of the issuer's public key, so it is assumed that this value is chosen by the issuer. As the same as it was discussed in Subsection 3.2, the worst case is that the issuer is malicious and that the issuer and the host platform are colluded. Therefore, an adversary plays the roles of a malicious issuer and host, and the adversary can deliberately choose the value p satisfying $p = uv + 1$, where $u \approx p^{1/3}$, and then mount the static DH attack by using a TPM as a static DH oracle and following the Brown-Gallant algorithm described in Section 2. Even if the issuer is not malicious and chooses a random p, an attacker can factorize $p - 1$ and apply the Brown-Gallant algorithm.

The above discussion shows that security of several ECC-DAA schemes is dependent on the hardness of the static DH problem. However, except [9, 20], the security of these schemes is proved under either the LRSW assumption or the SDH assumption, along with the decisional DH (DDH) assumption without mentioning the static DH assumption. By following a similar method as used in [6], in these security proofs, the simulator uses a random value to simulate the value K. It was argued that no adversary can distinguish the distribution of random K with distribution of K in the real system under the DDH assumption. However, again as we demonstrated before, instead of generating J by following the protocols and making it be the random distribution, the adversary can generate it by following the Brown-Gallant algorithm and then use a TPM as a static DH oracle. After that the adversary may benefit from the static DH attack. We believe that this information is missing in the security proofs of these ECC-DAA schemes as well.

5   Practical Impacts of Our Discovery

In this section, we discuss the practical impact to our discovery. We begin with impact to the RSA-DAA scheme [6] adopted in the TPM 1.2. In the parameters of the RSA-DAA scheme implemented in TPM 1.2, n (the RSA modulus) is 2048-bit, ρ (the order of $\mathbb{G}$) is 208-bit, Γ (the modulus of $\mathbb{G}$) is 1632-bit. It is generally believed that the RSA-DAA scheme has 104-bit security strength, i.e., it takes $O(2^{104})$ operations to break this DAA scheme.

By following our demonstration of the static DH attack, the RSA-DAA scheme in TPM 1.2 only offers around 70-bit of security in the worst case. The attack is as follows. Suppose ρ can be computed as $\rho = uv + 1$ such that u is 70-bit and v is 138-bit, then the attacker who compromised the host platform can make u (less than 2^{70}) signature queries to TPM and use $2(\sqrt{u} + \sqrt{v})$ (less than $2^{36} + 2^{70}$) modular exponentiations to extract the DAA private key. Observe that the $2(\sqrt{u} + \sqrt{v})$ modular exponentiations can be computed off-line in parallel, but the u static DH oracle queries to the TPM has to be run sequentially on the same TPM device. Also note that the TPM is very slow in computation. It may be more efficient to choose a smaller u, e.g., 50-bit u and 158-bit v, such that the attacker only needs to query the TPM 2^{50} times and compute roughly 2^{80} modular exponentiations to break the RSA-DAA scheme.

As we mentioned earlier in Section 3, if the issuer of the RSA-DAA scheme is corrupted, she can choose the DAA parameters including the ρ value. The issuer can choose a random 70-bit u and a random 138-bit v and compute $\rho = uv + 1$. The issuer then run the prime test, if ρ is not a prime number, she just repeats the previous step by choosing different u and v, until she finds a prime ρ. In this case, the security level of the RSA-DAA is downgraded to roughly 70-bit. If the issuer is trusted but following the RSA-DAA scheme to choose a random ρ. The security level of the RSA-DAA scheme depends on whether the attacker can factorize $\rho - 1$ and find appropriate u and v values to run the Brown-Gallant algorithm. Although integer factorization is a computationally hard problem, factorizing a 208-bit integer should be fairly easy with modern computers. A survey on integer factorization algorithms is given in [29]. Let l_ρ, l_u, l_v be the bit-size of ρ, u, v, respectively. If the attacker can find u such that $l_u \leq l_\rho/3$, then the attacker can break the RSA-DAA scheme with roughly $O(2^{(l_\rho - l_u)/2})$ operations. In other words, the security level of the RSA-DAA scheme becomes $(l_\rho - l_u)/2$ bits instead of $l_\rho/2$ bits.

For ECC-DAA schemes [7–9, 17, 18, 20, 21] which involved with a static DH oracle, the same attack and analysis above apply here. If a 256-bit elliptic curve is used as $\mathbb{G}$, the security strength of these ECC-DAA schemes can be as little as 85-bit, instead of 128-bit due to our discovery.

Note that the static DH problem is still believed to be a computationally hard problem, even with the Brown-Gallant attack. It is still far from being practical to break the DAA schemes [6–9, 17, 18, 20, 21] using the Brown-Gallant attack. Our discovery only shows that the security strength of these DAA schemes can be significantly weaken due to the static DH oracle used.

6   Mitigation Strategies

In this section, we provide two mitigation strategies as follows. The first mitigation is a simple fix, but may not be effective in certain situations. The second mitigation removes the dependency on the static DH assumption, thus protects future attacks on the static DH problem.

6.1 First Mitigation: Choose Safe Prime

For the DAA schemes that have already been deployed in the real systems, such as the RSA-DAA scheme in TPM 1.2, it is hard to modify the DAA signing algorithm on the field, since it may require firmware update to the TPM device. The easiest mitigation is to modify the issuer algorithm to choose ρ as a safe prime, i.e., $\rho = 2\rho' + 1$ where ρ and ρ' are both prime. Once the issuer publishes ρ as part of the DAA parameters, everyone can verify ρ is indeed a safe prime. The Brown-Gallant attack in Section 2 will not be effective, since the attacker cannot find a large u more than 2.

This mitigation method is effective for the RSA-DAA scheme [6]. However, for ECC-DAA schemes [7–9, 17, 18, 20, 21], it may not always be possible to choose ρ, the order of the elliptic curve, as a safe prime. It depends on how the elliptic curve is generated. It is pointed out in [13] that even for the standard NIST curves, it is possible to factorize $\rho - 1$ and find a reasonably large u. The ECC-DAA schemes [9, 17, 18, 20, 21] use elliptic curve group $\mathbb{G}_1$ with pairing capability as $\mathbb{G}$. The ECC-DAA schemes [7, 8] use $\mathbb{G}_T$ as $\mathbb{G}$. Many pairing-friendly curves have to be constructed in a special way. For example, the Barreto-Naehrig curves [3] are one of the few 128-bit security pairing friendly curves, and have the requirement that $\rho = 36w^4 + 36w^3 + 18w^2 + 6w + 1$ for some integer w. If ρ is 256-bit, then w is roughly 63-bit. Attacker can set $u = w$ and $v = 36w^3 + 36w^2 + 18w + 6$ and use u, v to perform the Brown-Gallant attack.

6.2 Second Mitigation: Avoid Static DH Assumption

The first mitigation above is simple, but may not work for all ECC-DAA schemes. In addition, the static DH assumption is relatively new to the research community. Brown and Gallant [13] have showed one algorithm to solve the static DH problem more efficient than the generic baby-step-giant-step algorithm for solving the discrete log problem. The static DH assumption has not been studied nearly enough to have confidence that more efficient algorithms will not be found. The safest mitigation is to modify the affected DAA schemes [6–9, 17, 18, 20, 21] to avoid the dependency on the static DH assumption.

In the RSA-DAA scheme [6], ζ is computed by the Host, either chosen randomly from the order ρ subgroup of $\mathbb{F}_\Gamma^*$ or computed as $(H_\Gamma(1\|\mathsf{bsn}_V))^{(\Gamma-1)/\rho}$ mod Γ, where bsn_V is the verifier's basename for deriving the base ρ. The Host sends ζ to the TPM who then verifies that ζ is indeed in the order ρ subgroup of $\mathbb{F}_\Gamma^*$, i.e., verifies that $\zeta^\rho \equiv 1 \pmod{\Gamma}$. To avoid the static DH assumption, we need to stop the TPM from acting as a static DH oracle. This can be done by letting the TPM compute ζ instead of the Host. Now, the TPM needs to compute optionally one hash H_Γ operation (if there is a basename involved) and one modular exponentiation on exponent $(\Gamma - 1)/\rho$ instead of computing a modular exponentiation on exponent ρ. Note that $(\Gamma - 1)/\rho$ is 1424-bit and ρ is only 208-bit using the recommended DAA parameters in TPM 1.2. This mitigation method requires significant more computation for the TPM.

In the ECC-DAA schemes [7–9, 17, 18, 20, 21], the Host computes J and the TPM computes $K = [f]J$, hence the TPM becomes a static DH oracle on f.

To avoid the static DH assumption, we can modify the ECC-DAA schemes such that both J and K are computed by the TPM. The value J in [9, 17, 18, 20, 21] is either randomly chosen or the result of a special hash function which hashes arbitrary messages to points on an elliptic curve. Computing J is usually cheaper than a point multiplication operation. This mitigation method only adds a small amount of computational overhead to the TPM.

7   Conclusion

We have demonstrated that many existing DAA schemes, including the original one adopted in TPM 1.2 specification and ISO/IEC 11889, can be used by a malicious user to treat a TPM as a static DH oracle and therefore security of these DAA schemes are relied on the hardness of the static DH problem. We have discussed that security proofs of most of these DAA schemes have not taken the feature of involving a static DH oracle into account. As a result, the claimed security strength of these DAA schemes is not accurate. By following the Brown-Gallant static DH attack algorithm, the security level of these schemes can be significantly weaken down to roughly 2/3 of the claimed security level. The paper aims to arise awareness of the connection between the TPM DAA implementation and the static DH assumption and to discuss how to patch the DAA schemes to enhance their security level and what the cost is needed. A formal security analysis of the suggested modification of these DAA schemes is listed as a future work.

References

1. ISO/IEC PAS DIS 11889: Information technology – Security techniques – Trusted platform module
2. Backes, M., Maffei, M., Unruh, D.: Zero-knowledge in the applied pi-calculus and automated verification of the direct anonymous attestation protocol. In: Proceedings of IEEE Symposium on Security and Privacy, pp. 202–215. IEEE Computer Society (2008)
3. Barreto, P.S.L.M., Naehrig, M.: Pairing-Friendly Elliptic Curves of Prime Order. In: Preneel, B., Tavares, S. (eds.) SAC 2005. LNCS, vol. 3897, pp. 319–331. Springer, Heidelberg (2006)
4. Bellare, M., Shi, H., Zhang, C.: Foundations of Group Signatures: The Case of Dynamic Groups. In: Menezes, A. (ed.) CT-RSA 2005. LNCS, vol. 3376, pp. 136–153. Springer, Heidelberg (2005)
5. Boneh, D., Boyen, X., Shacham, H.: Short Group Signatures. In: Franklin, M. (ed.) CRYPTO 2004. LNCS, vol. 3152, pp. 41–55. Springer, Heidelberg (2004)
6. Brickell, E., Camenisch, J., Chen, L.: Direct anonymous attestation. In: Proceedings of the 11th ACM Conference on Computer and Communications Security, pp. 132–145. ACM Press (2004)
7. Brickell, E., Chen, L., Li, J.: A New Direct Anonymous Attestation Scheme from Bilinear Maps. In: Lipp, P., Sadeghi, A.-R., Koch, K.-M. (eds.) Trust 2008. LNCS, vol. 4968, pp. 166–178. Springer, Heidelberg (2008)

8. Brickell, E., Chen, L., Li, J.: Simplified security notions of direct anonymous attestation and a concrete scheme from pairings. International Journal of Information Security 8(5), 315–330 (2009)

9. Brickell, E., Chen, L., Li, J.: A (Corrected) DAA Scheme Using Batch Proof and Verification. In: Chen, L., Yung, M., Zhu, L. (eds.) INTRUST 2011. LNCS, vol. 7222, pp. 304–337. Springer, Heidelberg (2012)

10. Brickell, E., Li, J.: Enhanced Privacy ID: A direct anonymous attestation scheme with enhanced revocation capabilities. In: Proceedings of the 6th ACM Workshop on Privacy in the Electronic Society, pp. 21–30 (October 2007)

11. Brickell, E., Li, J.: Enhanced Privacy ID from bilinear pairing for hardware authentication and attestation. In: Proceedings of 2nd IEEE International Conference on Information Privacy, Security, Risk and Trust, pp. 768–775 (2010)

12. Brickell, E., Li, J.: A Pairing-Based DAA Scheme Further Reducing TPM Resources. In: Acquisti, A., Smith, S.W., Sadeghi, A.-R. (eds.) TRUST 2010. LNCS, vol. 6101, pp. 181–195. Springer, Heidelberg (2010)

13. Brown, D.R.L., Gallant, R.P.: The static Diffie-Hellman problem. Cryptology ePrint Archive, Report 2004/306 (2004), http://eprint.iacr.org/

14. Camenisch, J.L., Lysyanskaya, A.: A Signature Scheme with Efficient Protocols. In: Cimato, S., Galdi, C., Persiano, G. (eds.) SCN 2002. LNCS, vol. 2576, pp. 268–289. Springer, Heidelberg (2003)

15. Camenisch, J.L., Lysyanskaya, A.: Signature Schemes and Anonymous Credentials from Bilinear Maps. In: Franklin, M. (ed.) CRYPTO 2004. LNCS, vol. 3152, pp. 56–72. Springer, Heidelberg (2004)

16. Chaum, D., van Antwerpen, H.: Undeniable Signatures. In: Brassard, G. (ed.) CRYPTO 1989. LNCS, vol. 435, pp. 212–216. Springer, Heidelberg (1990)

17. Chen, L.: A DAA Scheme Requiring Less TPM Resources. In: Bao, F., Yung, M., Lin, D., Jing, J. (eds.) Inscrypt 2009. LNCS, vol. 6151, pp. 350–365. Springer, Heidelberg (2010)

18. Chen, L.: A DAA Scheme Using Batch Proof and Verification. In: Acquisti, A., Smith, S.W., Sadeghi, A.-R. (eds.) TRUST 2010. LNCS, vol. 6101, pp. 166–180. Springer, Heidelberg (2010)

19. Chen, L., Morrissey, P., Smart, N.P.: Pairings in Trusted Computing. In: Galbraith, S.D., Paterson, K.G. (eds.) Pairing 2008. LNCS, vol. 5209, pp. 1–17. Springer, Heidelberg (2008)

20. Chen, L., Morrissey, P., Smart, N.P.: DAA: Fixing the pairing based protocols. Cryptology ePrint Archive, Report 2009/198 (2009), http://eprint.iacr.org/

21. Chen, L., Page, D., Smart, N.P.: On the Design and Implementation of an Efficient DAA Scheme. In: Gollmann, D., Lanet, J.-L., Iguchi-Cartigny, J. (eds.) CARDIS 2010. LNCS, vol. 6035, pp. 223–237. Springer, Heidelberg (2010)

22. Chen, X., Feng, D.: Direct anonymous attestation for next generation TPM. Journal of Computers 3(12), 43–50 (2008)

23. Cheon, J.H.: Security Analysis of the Strong Diffie-Hellman Problem. In: Vaudenay, S. (ed.) EUROCRYPT 2006. LNCS, vol. 4004, pp. 1–11. Springer, Heidelberg (2006)

24. El Gamal, T.: A Public Key Cryptosystem and a Signature Scheme Based on Discrete Logarithms. In: Blakely, G.R., Chaum, D. (eds.) CRYPTO 1984. LNCS, vol. 196, pp. 10–18. Springer, Heidelberg (1985)

25. Ford, W., Kaliski, B.S.: Server-assisted generation of a strong secret from a password. In: Proceedings of the IEEE 9th International Workshops on Enabling Technologies: Infrastructure for Collaborative Enterprises, pp. 176–180 (2000)

26. Ge, H., Tate, S.R.: A Direct Anonymous Attestation Scheme for Embedded Devices. In: Okamoto, T., Wang, X. (eds.) PKC 2007. LNCS, vol. 4450, pp. 16–30. Springer, Heidelberg (2007)
27. Lysyanskaya, A., Rivest, R.L., Sahai, A., Wolf, S.: Pseudonym Systems (Extended Abstract). In: Heys, H.M., Adams, C.M. (eds.) SAC 1999. LNCS, vol. 1758, pp. 184–199. Springer, Heidelberg (2000)
28. Menezes, A.J., Oorschot, P.C.V., Vanstone, S.A.: Handbook of Applied Cryptography (revised reprint with updates). CRC Press (1997)
29. Montgomery, P.L.: A survey of modern integer factorization algorithms. CWI Quarterly 7, 337–366 (1994)
30. Trusted Computing Group. TCG TPM specification 1.2 (2003), http://www.trustedcomputinggroup.org

Appendix A

In the appendix, we recall the DAA-Join (as shown in Figure 1) and DAA-Sign (as shown in Figure 2) protocols in the original RSA-DAA scheme in [6]. We first employ the security parameters: ℓ_n (2048) is the size of the RSA modulus, ℓ_f (104) is the size of the f_i's (information encoded into the certificate), ℓ_e (368) is the size of the e's (exponents, part of certificate), ℓ_e' (120) is the size of the interval that the e's are chosen from, ℓ_v (2536) is the size of the v's (random value, part of certificate), $\ell_\varnothing$ (80) is the security parameter controlling the statistical zero-knowledge property, $\ell_\mathcal{H}$ (160) is the output length of the hash function used for the Fiat-Shamir heuristic, ℓ_r (80) is the security parameter needed for the reduction in the proof of security, ℓ_s (1024) is the size to split large exponent for easier computations on the TPM, ℓ_Γ (1632) is the size of the modulus Γ, and ℓ_ρ (208) is the size of the order ρ of the sub group of $\mathbb{Z}_\Gamma^*$ that is used for rogue-tagging (the numbers in parentheses are our proposal for these parameters). We require that: $\ell_e > \ell_\varnothing + \ell_\mathcal{H} + \max\{\ell_f + 4 , \ell_e' + 2\}$, $\ell_v > \ell_n + \ell_\varnothing + \ell_\mathcal{H} + \max\{\ell_f + \ell_r + 3 , \ell_\varnothing + 2\}$, and $\ell_\rho = 2\ell_f$.

The DAA issuer's parameters are created with the following steps:

1. The issuer chooses a RSA modulus $n = pq$ with $p = 2p' + 1$, $q = 2q' + 1$ such that p, p', q, q' are all primes and n has ℓ_n bits. Furthermore, it chooses a random generator g' of QR_n (the group of quadratic residues modulo n).
2. Next, it chooses random integers $x_0, x_1, x_z, x_s, x_h, x_g \in [1, p'q']$ and computes

$$g := g'^{x_g} \bmod n, \quad h := g'^{x_h} \bmod n, \quad S := h^{x_s} \bmod n,$$
$$Z := h^{x_z} \bmod n, \quad R_0 := S^{x_0} \bmod n, \quad R_1 := S^{x_1} \bmod n.$$

   It produces a non-interactive proof *proof* that R_0, R_1, S, Z, g, and h are computed correctly, i.e., that $g, h \in \langle g' \rangle$, $S, Z \in \langle h \rangle$, and $R_0, R_1 \in \langle S \rangle$.
3. It generates a group of prime order: Choose random primes ρ and Γ such that $\Gamma = r\rho + 1$ for some r with $\rho \nmid r$, $2^{\ell_\Gamma - 1} < \Gamma < 2^{\ell_\Gamma}$, and $2^{\ell_\rho - 1} < \rho < 2^{\ell_\rho}$. Choose a random $\gamma' \in_R \mathbb{Z}_\Gamma^*$ such that $\gamma'^{(\Gamma-1)/\rho} \not\equiv 1 \pmod{\Gamma}$ and set $\gamma := \gamma'^{(\Gamma-1)/\rho} \bmod \Gamma$.

The DAA-Join protocol works as follows.

1. The host computes $\zeta_I := (H_\Gamma(1\|\mathbf{bsn}_I))^{(\Gamma-1)/\rho} \bmod \Gamma$ and sends ζ_I to the TPM.
2. The TPM checks whether $\zeta_I^\rho \equiv 1 \pmod{\Gamma}$. The TPM computes

$$f := H(H(\mathtt{DAAseed}\|H(PK_I'))\|\mathtt{cnt}\|0)\| \ H(H(\mathtt{DAAseed}\|H(PK_I'))\|\mathtt{cnt}\|1) \mod \rho,$$

$$f_0 := \mathtt{LSB}_{\ell_f}(f) \ , \quad f_1 := \mathtt{CAR}_{\ell_f}(f) \ , \quad v' \in_R \{0,1\}^{\ell_n+\ell_\varnothing} \ ,$$

$$U := R_0^{f_0} R_1^{f_1} S^{v'} \bmod n \ , \quad N_I := \zeta_I^{f_0+f_1 2^{\ell_f}} \bmod \Gamma$$

and sends U and N_I to the host who forwards to the issuer.
3. The issuer checks for all (f_0, f_1) on the rogue list whether $N_I \overset{?}{\not\equiv} (\zeta_I^{f_0+f_1 2^{\ell_f}})$ $(\bmod\ \Gamma)$. The issuer also checks this for the N_I this platform had used previously. If the issuer finds the platform to be rogue, it aborts the protocol.
4. The TPM proves to the issuer knowledge of f_0, f_1, and v': it executes as prover the protocol

$$SPK\{(f_0, f_1, v') : \quad U \equiv \pm R_0^{f_0} R_1^{f_1} S^{v'} \pmod{n} \ \wedge \ N_I \equiv \zeta_I^{f_0+f_1 2^{\ell_f}} \pmod{\Gamma} \ \wedge$$

$$f_0, f_1 \in \{0,1\}^{\ell_f+\ell_\varnothing+\ell_\mathcal{H}+2} \ \wedge \ v' \in \{0,1\}^{\ell_n+\ell_\varnothing+\ell_\mathcal{H}+2}\}(n_t\|n_i)$$

with the issuer as the verifier. This protocol is implemented as follows, where some non-critical operations are performed by the host and not be the TPM.
   (a) The TPM picks random integers $r_{f_0}, r_{f_1} \in_R \{0,1\}^{\ell_f+\ell_\varnothing+\ell_\mathcal{H}}$ and $r_{v'}$ $\in_R \{0,1\}^{\ell_n+2\ell_\varnothing+\ell_\mathcal{H}}$, computes $\tilde{U} := R_0^{r_{f_0}} R_1^{r_{f_1}} S^{r_{v'}} \bmod n$ and $\tilde{N}_I :=$ $\zeta_I^{r_{f_0}+r_{f_1} 2^{\ell_f}} \bmod \Gamma$, and sends $\tilde{U}$ and $\tilde{N}_I$ to the host.
   (b) The issuer chooses a random string $n_i \in \{0,1\}^{\ell_\mathcal{H}}$ and sends n_i to the host.
   (c) The host computes $c_h := H(n\|R_0\|R_1\|S\|U\|N_I\|\tilde{U}\|\tilde{N}_I\|n_i)$ and sends c_h to the TPM.
   (d) The TPM chooses a random $n_t \in \{0,1\}^{\ell_\varnothing}$ and computes $c := H(c_h\|n_t) \in [0, 2^{\ell_\mathcal{H}} - 1]$.
   (e) The TPM computes $s_{f_0} := r_{f_0} + c \cdot f_0$, $s_{f_1} := r_{f_1} + c \cdot f_1$, and $s_{v'} := r_{v'} + c \cdot v'$ and sends the host $(c, n_t, s_{f_0}, s_{f_1}, s_{v'})$.
   (f) The host forwards $(c, n_t, s_{f_0}, s_{f_1}, s_{v'})$ to the issuer.
   (g) The issuer verifies the proof by computing $\hat{U} := U^{-c} R_0^{s_{f_0}} R_1^{s_{f_1}} S^{s_{v'}} \bmod n$ and $\hat{N}_I := N_I^{-c} \zeta_I^{s_{f_0}+2^{\ell_f} s_{f_1}} \bmod \Gamma$ and checking if $c \overset{?}{=} H(H(n\|R_0\|R_1\|$ $S\|U\|N_I\|\hat{U}\|\hat{N}_I\|n_i)\|n_t)$, $s_{f_0}, s_{f_1} \overset{?}{\in} \{0,1\}^{\ell_f+\ell_\varnothing+\ell_\mathcal{H}+1}$, and $s_{v'} \overset{?}{\in}$ $\{0,1\}^{\ell_n+2\ell_\varnothing+\ell_\mathcal{H}+1}$.
5. The issuer chooses $\hat{v} \in_R \{0,1\}^{\ell_v-1}$ and a prime $e \in_R [2^{\ell_e-1}, 2^{\ell_e-1}+2^{\ell_e'-1}]$ and computes $v'' := \hat{v} + 2^{\ell_v-1}$ and

$$A := \left(\frac{Z}{US^{v''}}\right)^{1/e} \bmod n \ .$$

6. To convince the host that A was correctly computed, the issuer as prover runs the protocol

$$SPK\{(d) : \quad A \equiv \pm\left(\frac{Z}{US^{v''}}\right)^d \pmod{n}\}(n_h)$$

with the host:
   (a) The host chooses a random integer $n_h \in \{0,1\}^{\ell_\varnothing}$ and sends n_h to the issuer.
   (b) The issuer randomly chooses $r_e \in_R [0, p'q']$, computes $\tilde{A} := \left(\frac{Z}{US^{v''}}\right)^{r_e} \bmod n$, $c' := H(n\|Z\|S\|U\|v''\|A\|\tilde{A}\|n_h)$, and $s_e := r_e - c'/e \bmod p'q'$, and sends c', s_e, and (A, e, v'') to the host.
   (c) The host verifies whether e is a prime and lies in $[2^{\ell_e-1}, 2^{\ell_e-1} + 2^{\ell_e'-1}]$, computes $\hat{A} := A^{c'}\left(\frac{Z}{US^{v''}}\right)^{s_e} \bmod n$, and checks whether $c' \overset{?}{=}$ $H(n\|Z\|S\|U\|v''\|A\|\hat{A}\|n_h)$.
7. The host forwards v'' to the TPM.
8. The TPM receives v'', sets $v := v'' + v'$, and stores (f_0, f_1, v).

Fig. 1. The DAA-Join protocol. The inputs to the TPM are $(n, R_0, R_1, S, \rho, \Gamma)$, $\mathtt{DAAseed}$, $\mathtt{cnt}$, $H(PK_I')$, the input to the host is $(n, R_0, R_1, S, Z, \rho, \Gamma)$, and the input to the issuer are $(n, R_0, R_1, S, Z, \rho, \Gamma)$, p and q.

The DAA-Sign protocol works as follows.

1. (a) Depending on the verifier's request (i.e., whether $\mathbf{bsn}_V \neq \bot$ or not), the host computes ζ as follows

$$\zeta \in_R \langle \gamma \rangle \qquad \text{or} \qquad \zeta := (H_\Gamma(1\|\mathbf{bsn}_V))^{(\Gamma-1)/\rho} \bmod \Gamma$$

and sends ζ to the TPM.
   (b) The TPM checks whether $\zeta^\rho \equiv 1 \pmod{\Gamma}$.
2. (a) The host picks random integers $w, r \in \{0,1\}^{\ell_n + \ell_\varnothing}$ and computes $T_1 := Ah^w \bmod n$ and $T_2 := g^w h^e (g')^r \bmod n$.
   (b) The TPM computes $N_V := \zeta^{f_0 + f_1 2^{\ell_f}} \bmod \Gamma$ and sends N_V to the host.
3. Now, the TPM and host together produce a "signature of knowledge" that T_1 and T_2 commit to a certificate and N_V was computed using the secret key going with that certificate. That is, they compute the "signature of knowledge"

$$SPK\{(f_0, f_1, v, e, w, r, ew, ee, er):$$

$$Z \equiv \pm T_1^e R_0^{f_0} R_1^{f_1} S^v h^{-ew} \pmod{n} \ \wedge \ T_2 \equiv \pm g^w h^e g'^r \pmod{n} \ \wedge$$

$$1 \equiv \pm T_2^{-e} g^{ew} h^{ee} g'^{er} \pmod{n} \ \wedge \ N_V \equiv \zeta^{f_0 + f_1 2^{\ell_f}} \pmod{\Gamma} \ \wedge$$

$$f_0, f_1 \in \{0,1\}^{\ell_f + \ell_\varnothing + \ell_{\mathcal{H}} + 2} \ \wedge \ (e - 2^{\ell_e}) \in \{0,1\}^{\ell'_e + \ell_\varnothing + \ell_{\mathcal{H}} + 1}\}(n_t \| n_v \| b \| m) \ .$$

Most of the secrets involved are actually known by the host; in fact only the values involving f_0, f_1, and v need to be computed by the TPM, as the reader can see below.

(a) i. The TPM picks random integers $r_v \in_R \{0,1\}^{\ell_v + \ell_\varnothing + \ell_{\mathcal{H}}}$ and $r_{f_0}, r_{f_1} \in_R \{0,1\}^{\ell_f + \ell_\varnothing + \ell_{\mathcal{H}}}$ and computes

$$\tilde{T}_{1t} := R_0^{r_{f_0}} R_1^{r_{f_1}} S^{r_v} \bmod n \quad \tilde{r}_f := r_{f_0} + r_{f_1} 2^{\ell_f} \bmod \rho \quad \tilde{N}_V := \zeta^{\tilde{r}_f} \bmod \Gamma \ .$$

The TPM sends $\tilde{T}_{1t}$ and $\tilde{N}_V$ to the host.
   ii. The host picks random integers

$$r_e \in_R \{0,1\}^{\ell'_e + \ell_\varnothing + \ell_{\mathcal{H}}} \ , \qquad r_{ee} \in_R \{0,1\}^{2\ell_e + \ell_\varnothing + \ell_{\mathcal{H}} + 1} \ ,$$

$$r_w, r_r \in_R \{0,1\}^{\ell_n + 2\ell_\varnothing + \ell_{\mathcal{H}}} \ , \qquad r_{ew}, r_{er} \in_R \{0,1\}^{\ell_e + \ell_n + 2\ell_\varnothing + \ell_{\mathcal{H}} + 1}$$

and computes

$$\tilde{T}_1 := \tilde{T}_{1t} T_1^{r_e} h^{-r_{ew}} \bmod n, \ \tilde{T}_2 := g^{r_w} h^{r_e} g'^{r_r} \bmod n \ ,$$

$$\tilde{T}'_2 := T_2^{-r_e} g^{r_{ew}} h^{r_{ee}} g'^{r_{er}} \bmod n \ .$$

(b) i. Host computes $c_h := H((n\|g\|g'\|h\|R_0\|R_1\|S\|Z\|\gamma\|\Gamma\|\rho)\|\zeta\|(T_1\|T_2)\|N_V\| (\tilde{T}_1\|\tilde{T}_2\|\tilde{T}'_2)\|\tilde{N}_V)\|n_v) \in [0, 2^{\ell_{\mathcal{H}}} - 1]$, and sends c_h to the TPM.
   ii. The TPM chooses a random $n_t \in \{0,1\}^{\ell_\varnothing}$, computes $c := H(H(c_h\|n_t)\|b\|m)$, and sends c, n_t to the host.

(c) i. The TPM computes (over the integers)

$$s_v := r_v + c \cdot v \ , \quad s_{f_0} := r_{f_0} + c \cdot f_0 \ , \quad \text{and} \quad s_{f_1} := r_{f_1} + c \cdot f_1$$

and sends (s_v, s_{f_0}, s_{f_1}) to the host.
   ii. The host computes (over the integers)

$$s_e := r_e + c \cdot (e - 2^{\ell_e - 1}) \ , \quad s_{ee} := r_{ee} + c \cdot e^2 \ , \quad s_w := r_w + c \cdot w \ ,$$

$$s_{ew} := r_{ew} + c \cdot w \cdot e \ , \qquad s_r := r_r + c \cdot r \ , \qquad s_{er} := r_{er} + c \cdot e \cdot r \ .$$

4. The host outputs the signature $\sigma := (\zeta, (T_1, T_2), N_V, c, n_t, (s_v, s_{f_0}, s_{f_1}, s_e, s_{ee}, s_w, s_{ew}, s_r, s_{er}))$.

Fig. 2. The DAA-Sign protocol. The input to the protocol for the TPM is m, $(n, R_0, R_1, S, \Gamma, \rho)$, and (f_0, f_1, v), and the host's input to the protocol is m, the certificate (A, e) and $(n, g, g', h, R_0, R_1, S, Z, \gamma, \Gamma, \rho)$.

4. Finally, it publishes the public key $(n, g', g, h, S, Z, R_0, R_1, \gamma, \Gamma, \rho)$ along with its proof *proof* (see [6] for the details of the proof) and stores $p'q'$ as its secret key.

Note that the issuer is required to choose a random prime for the value ρ, but there is no proof whether the issuer does it correctly or not.

Finally, let $H_\Gamma(\cdot)$ and $H(\cdot)$ be two collision resistant hash functions $H_\Gamma(\cdot)$: $\{0,1\}^* \to \{0,1\}^{\ell_\Gamma + \ell_\varnothing}$ and $H(\cdot) : \{0,1\}^* \to \{0,1\}^{\ell_\mathcal{H}}$.

The Yin and Yang Sides of Embedded Security
(Extended Abstract)

Christof Paar

Horst Görtz Institute for IT-Security
Ruhr-Universität Bochum
www.emsec.rub.de

1 Introduction

Through the prevalence of interconnected embedded systems, the vision of ubiquitous computing has become reality over the last few years. As part of this development, embedded security has become an increasingly important issue in a multitude of applications. Examples include the Stuxnet virus, which has allegedly delayed the Iranian nuclear program, killer applications in the consumer area like iTunes or Amazon's Kindle (the business models of which rely heavily on IP protection) and even medical implants like pace makers and insulin pumps that allow remote configuration. These examples show the destructive and constructive aspects of modern embedded security. The Eastern concept of of yin and yang can be useful for explaining these seemingly contradicting aspects (quote taken from Wikipedia):

> The concept of yin yang is used to describe how polar opposites or seemingly contrary forces are interconnected and interdependent in the natural world, and how they give rise to each other in turn.

In this contribution, we will present some of our research projects over the last few years which dealt with both the yin and yang aspect of embedded security. We look at securing future car communication and lightweight security for the Internet of Things. As "yang example" of our research we will show how two devices with very large deployment in the real world can be broken, namely the voice encryption of satellite phones and the design security features of FPGAs.

2 High-Speed (but Low-Cost) Cryptography for Car2X Communication

In 1–2 generations of automobiles, car2car and car2infrastructure communication will be available for driver-assistance and comfort applications. The emerging car2x standards, especially the IEEE 1609.2 standard which is the most developed standard at the time of writing, call for strong security functionality. The large number of data from up to several 1000 incoming messages per second, the

C.J. Mitchell and A. Tomlinson (Eds.): INTRUST 2012, LNCS 7711, pp. 112–115, 2012.
© Springer-Verlag Berlin Heidelberg 2012

strict cost constraints, and the embedded environment makes this a challenging task. At the same time, due to the long life expectancy of moderns cars, long-term security is required. We show how an extremely high-performance digital signature engine was realized using low-cost FPGAs [3]. Our signature engine is currently widely used in field trials in the USA.

3   Lightweight Security for the Internet of Things

The next case study addresses the other end of the performance spectrum, namely lightweight cryptography. In recent years more and more security sensitive applications use passive smart devices such as contactless smart cards and RFID tags. One particular problem of such passive devices are the harsh power constraints. Other constrains include energy and cost. As a result of this situation, research on block ciphers, an area that had almost come to a standstill after the completion of the AES selection process, has undergone a renaissance with the goal of developing lightweight algorithms which are suited for extremely area and energy constrained platforms like RFID tags. Such *domain-specific ciphers* are an important emerging area within applied cryptography. We describe the development of PRESENT [1], one of the smallest known ciphers which can be realized with as few as 1000 gates. The cipher was designed for extremely constrained applications, e.g., contactless smart cards or RFID tags. The latter can be used, e.g., as a tool for anti-counterfeiting of spare parts, or for other low-power applications. PRESENT has recently been standardized as ISO/IEC 29192-2:2012, Information technology – Security techniques.

4   The Insecurity of Current Satellite Phone Standards

There is a rich body of literature related to the security aspects of mobile phones, in particular with respect to the GSM and UMTS systems. However, until our recent contribution in [2], there was no investigation about the security of satellite phones, or satphones. Even though a niche market compared to the G2 and G3 mobile system, there are several 100,000 satphone subscribers worldwide. Given the sensitive nature of some of their application domains, e.g., natural disaster areas or military campaigns, security plays arguably a particular important role for satphones.

We analyzed the voice-encryption systems used in the two existing (and competing) satphone standards, GMR-1 and GMR-2. The first main finding is that we were able to completely reverse engineer the respective voice encryption algorithms employed. Both ciphers had not been publicly known previously. The two algorithms were recovered from freely available DSP-firmware updates for satphones. This process included the development of a disassembler and tools to analyze the code, and extending prior work on binary analysis to efficiently identify cryptographic code. We note that these steps had to be repeated for both systems, because the available binaries were from two entirely different DSP processors. Perhaps somewhat surprisingly, it was found that the GMR-1 cipher can be considered a proprietary variant of the GSM A5/2 algorithm, whereas the GMR-2 cipher is an entirely new design. The second main contribution lies in the cryptanalysis of the two proprietary stream ciphers. We were able to adopt known A5/2 ciphertext-only attacks to the GMR-1 algorithm with an average case complexity of 2^{32} steps. With respect to the GMR-2 cipher, we developed a new attack which is powerful in a known-plaintext setting. In this situation, the encryption key for one session, i.e., one phone call, can be recovered with approximately 50–65 bytes of key stream and a moderate computational complexity. A major finding of our work is that the stream ciphers of the two existing satellite phone systems are considerably weaker than what is state-of-the-art in symmetric cryptography.

5   Overcoming FPGA "Security" Features

The second attack breaks the bit stream encryption of current FPGAs, which are programmable hardware ICs. The combine the flexibility of software solutions with the speed of application specific integrated circuits. Over the last two decades FPGAs have become central components for many advanced digital systems, e.g., video signal processing, network routers, data acquisition and military systems. In order to protect the intellectual property and to prevent fraud, e.g., by cloning a design embedded into an FPGA or manipulating its content, many current FPGAs employ a bitstream encryption feature. We develop a successful attack on the bitstream encryption engine integrated in the widespread Virtex-II Pro FPGAs from Xilinx, using side-channel analysis. After measuring the power consumption of a single power-up of the device and a modest amount of on-line computation, we are able to recover all three different keys used by its triple DES module. Our method allows extracting secret keys from any real-world device where the bitstream encryption feature of Virtex-II Pro is enabled. As a consequence, the target product can be cloned and manipulated at the will of the attacker since no side-channel protection was included into the design of the decryption module. Also, more advanced attacks such as reverse engineering or the introduction of hardware Trojans become potential threats. While performing the side-channel attack, we were able to deduce a hypothetical architecture of the hardware encryption engine. To our knowledge, this is the first attack against the bitstream encryption of a commercial FPGA reported in the open literature. Details of the attack are described in [4,5].

Acknowledgment. I would like to thank the following colleagues, who conducted much of the research that is summarized in this contribution: Alessandro Barenghi, Andrey Bogdanov, Benedikt Driessen, Tim Güneysu, Lars Knudsen, Thorsten Holz, Ralf Hund, Markus Kasper, Timo Kasper, Amir Moradi, Axel Poschmann, Matt Robshaw and Carsten Willems.

References

1. Bogdanov, A., Knudsen, L.R., Leander, G., Paar, C., Poschmann, A., Robshaw, M.J.B., Seurin, Y., Vikkelsoe, C.: PRESENT: An Ultra-Lightweight Block Cipher. In: Paillier, P., Verbauwhede, I. (eds.) CHES 2007. LNCS, vol. 4727, pp. 450–466. Springer, Heidelberg (2007)
2. Driessen, B., Hund, R., Willems, C., Paar, C., Holz, T.: Don't trust satellite phones: A security analysis of two satphone standards. In: IEEE Symposium on Security and Privacy, pp. 128–142 (2012)
3. Güneysu, T., Paar, C.: Ultra High Performance ECC over NIST Primes on Commercial FPGAs. In: Oswald, E., Rohatgi, P. (eds.) CHES 2008. LNCS, vol. 5154, pp. 62–78. Springer, Heidelberg (2008)
4. Moradi, A., Barenghi, A., Kasper, T., Paar, C.: On the Vulnerability of FPGA Bitstream Encryption against Power Analysis Attacks: Extracting keys from Xilinx Virtex-II FPGAs. In: Chen, Y., Danezis, G., Shmatikov, V. (eds.) ACM Conference on Computer and Communications Security (CCS 2011), pp. 111–124 (2011)
5. Moradi, A., Kasper, M., Paar, C.: Black-Box Side-Channel Attacks Highlight the Importance of Countermeasures. In: Dunkelman, O. (ed.) CT-RSA 2012. LNCS, vol. 7178, pp. 1–18. Springer, Heidelberg (2012)

Author Index